Old Russia in Modern America

*Living Traditions
of the Russian Old Believers*

Alexander B. Dolitsky

Alaska–Siberia Research Center
P.O. Box 34871
Juneau, Alaska 99803

2017

Published by the Alaska–Siberia Research Center (AKSRC), Juneau, Alaska (with assistance and additional funding provided by the Shared Beringian Heritage Program, U.S. National Park Service, Anchorage, Alaska). 2017.

Fourth updated and revised edition
The first two editions were published in 1991 and 1994 by the Alaska–Siberia Research Center (AKSRC) under the title *Change, Stability, and Values in the World of Culture: A Case from Russian Old Believers in Alaska*. The 3rd edition was published by AKSRC in 1998 under the title *Old Russia in Modern America: A Case from Russian Old Believers in Alaska*.

Front illustration: A fragment of the historical painting of the Russian Old Believer, *Boyarynya Morozova*, taken to be burned at the stake in the mid-17th century. The painting, by Vasiliy Surikov in 1887, is in the collection of the Moscow Tretyakov Gallery. The painting *Boyarynya Morozova* depicts the defiant *boyarynya* who was arrested by tsarist authorities in 1671. She holds two fingers raised: a hint of the old (i.e., "proper") way.

Back illustration: Anisim Kalugin and his wife Solomeya, Nikolaevsk, AK, May 1986. Photo by Alexander Dolitsky.

Printed and bound by AMICA, Inc.
Printed in China
Includes bibliographical references and index
General editor and production manager: *Alexander B. Dolitsky*, AKSRC, Juneau, AK
Copy editors: *Linda E. Kruger, James F. Gebhardt* and *Ian Buvit*
Proof reader: *Miriam Lancaster*
Book designer: *Andy Romanoff*, Alaska Litho, Inc., Juneau, AK
Cover designer: *Andy Romanoff*, Alaska Litho, Inc., Juneau, AK

Hardbound edition: ISBN 10: 0-9653891-9-7; ISBN 13: 978-0-9653891-9-8

Key words: Russian Old Believers, Russian Orthodox Church Schism, Alaska, Siberia, cultural change, cultural continuity, cultural stability, living memory, living tradition.

The paper in this book meets the guidelines for permanence and durability of the Committee on Production Guidelines for Book Longevity of the Council on Library Resources.

Russian Old Believers in Alaska

Updated and Revised Edition

TABLE OF CONTENTS

TRANSLITERATION TABLE

The system of transliteration adopted in this work is that of the United States Board of Geographic Names, with slight modifications for technical reasons. Instead of e, we use ye at the beginning of names, after vowels and after the soft sign (ь), or yo (ё) where e is accented as ё. The soft sign (ь) and hard sign (ъ) have no sound value but they soften or harden the sound of the letter in front of them. A hard sign (ъ) is transliterated when in the middle of a word and disregarded when final.

Russian Letters		Transliteration	
А	а	a	(as in star, car, Arkansas)
Б	б	b	(as in boots, Bill, Britain)
В	в	v	(as in voice, Virginia)
Г	г	g	(as in go, good, Michigan)
Д	д	d	(as in do, road, Dakota)
Е	е	ye	(as in met, yes)
Ё	ё	yo	(as in yonder, York)
Ж	ж	zh	(as in pleasure)
З	з	z	(as in zoo, is, Kansas)
И	и	i	(as in meet, seat)
Й	й	y	(as in may, boy)
К	к	k	(as in cat, kind, Kentucky)
Л	л	l	(as in belt, lion, Florida)
М	м	m	(as in amuse, mother, Mexico)
Н	н	n	(as in now, noose, Nebraska)
О	о	o	(as in port, comb, Oklahoma)
П	п	p	(as in pure, poor, Portland)
Р	р	r	(as in river, trilled, Arizona)
С	с	s	(as in swim, SOS, South)
Т	т	t	(as in stool, tiger, Texas)
У	у	u	(as in lunar, tune)
Ф	ф	f	(as in food, funny, California)
Х	х	kh	(as in Loch Ness)
Ц	ц	ts	(as in its, quartz, waltz)
Ч	ч	ch	(as in cheap, chain, cheese)
Ш	ш	sh	(as in fish, sheep, shrimp)
Щ	щ	shch	(as in borshch)
Ъ	ъ	"	(hard sign; no equivalent)
Ы	ы	y	(as in rip, flip)
Ь	ь	'	(soft sign; no equivalent)
Э	э	e	(as in best, chest, effort)
Ю	ю	yu	(as in you, Yukon)
Я	я	ya	(as in yard, yahoo)

FOREWORD

As social scientists, anthropologists attempt to formulate theories that help us understand and compare societies and their cultures. These theories must be tested and evaluated against the data through field investigation or historical research. This testing of theories is critical in the areas of culture change and applied anthropology, where government agencies try to assist those undergoing socio-cultural change resulting from external pressure by dominant cultures. Efforts may fail and large amounts of resources can be wasted on projects based on a flawed or otherwise inaccurate theory.

Some early theories in anthropology and philosophy, such as unilineal evolution, have proven to be inadequate and even misleading.[1] We now know that societies do not progress through the same stages of cultural change. Structural-functional theories emphasize the integration of culture by showing how technology and economics, social and political systems, and beliefs and values influence each other. According to this way of looking at societies, as one part of the system changes, such as the economic condition, the social organization and religion will eventually adjust to the new situation.

Recent research shows that societies respond to new situations, experiences, or challenges in various ways. For example, in the United States we say that our goal is to have all citizens assimilate or blend into a cohesive socio-economic union, commonly known as the "melting pot" society.[2] But, in fact, many ethnic and religious groups have not "melted" into the mainstream. In reality, prejudice and discrimination against ethnic and religious minorities have been widespread in the United States. The truth is that many people have been denied access to the benefits of life in America. Throughout the history of this country, we have demanded that our indigenous peoples—American Indians and Alaska Natives—give up their land, their traditional hunting, fishing, farming, subsistence activities, their family life, their beliefs and rites for a "more civilized way." Missionaries and government agencies have worked hard to eradicate many of the ancient traditions and cultures in the Arctic, a vast region shared by the circumpolar countries.[3] But what has this policy done for these people besides leave them much worse off than before? In response, some groups have preferred to keep themselves separate from the dominant society; and some groups feel that they benefit much more from their separatism than by abandoning their traditional ways.

---

1 Editor's note: A unilineal evolution is following a single and consistent path of development or progression [Dolitsky].

2 Editor's note: A "melting pot" is a country, place or region in which immigrants of various nationalities and races are assimilated with a dominant culture [Dolitsky].

3 Editor's note: Under the United Nations' Environmental Protection Program, the southern limit of the Arctic region is generally maintained north of the 60th parallel, as defined by the eight circumpolar countries—Canada, USA, Russia, Denmark, Sweden, Finland, Greenland, Norway, and Iceland [Dolitsky].

The case of the Russian Orthodox Old Believers highlights the importance that people place on their beliefs, worship practices, and traditions. Old Believers find strength and security in their belief that they are following God's plan. Outsiders may look at them as unusual or "backward" and try to force them into a new lifestyle that conforms with the dominant society. In response, Old Believers have established what is known in modern anthropological theory as "boundary-maintaining systems." That is, they have found ways to keep themselves separate and distinct from the dominant society. People build social boundaries by maintaining and preserving their own native language, appearance, foods and, most of all, their own traditional religious beliefs and practices.

In the past, Russian Old Believers took the only option left to them if they wished to keep their faith and practices—they moved to new and remote locations. They fled their homeland to avoid persecution by hostile neighbors and oppressive governments. Some have remained in the former Soviet Union's republics while others moved to the United States—Oregon and Alaska. The latter are a vivid example of people who are willing to give up nearly everything for their religious principles and cultural traditions. In Alaska, some feel that they have finally found a home.

The following monograph by Alexander Dolitsky is a valuable contribution to the research on Alaska and the circumpolar region for two main reasons. First, it provides a fine ethnohistorical description of the Russian Orthodox Old Believers in contemporary Alaska. This part of the work gives us an insight into why the Old Believers came to Alaska and why they want to continue their traditional and religious way of life. Second, the book clarifies and modifies aspects of the theories regarding socio-cultural change in the Arctic and circumpolar regions.

The importance of this study extends beyond the Russian Old Believers; it has implications for indigenous peoples across the Arctic and circumpolar region, and beyond. The drive of dominant cultures to transform others by attacking and insulting their traditional cultures, with the dominant cultures values and beliefs, has resulted in social and psychological disaster in many regions of the world, including our own state—Alaska. The process has been based on the false assumption that the dominant and technologically advanced culture is superior to all others. What we have to face and recognize in our public policy and planning is that we live in a pluralistic society in which we must respect the rights and cultural traditions of all people, even if they are distinctly different from our own.

There is beauty in diversity. On our national coinage is the inscription *E pluribus Unum*—from many to one. In theory and practice, while seeking unity, we should not fail to respect the rights of those who prefer to follow their traditional religious beliefs and practices.

Wallace M. Olson
University of Alaska Southeast, Juneau, Alaska

PREFACE

Profoundly religious, the Russian people were shaken to their core by the Russian Orthodox Church liturgical reforms introduced by Patriarch Nikon (1666–1667) who, under the reign of Tsar Alexis Mikhailovich Romanov (1645–1676), had dared to correct the mistakes in the manuscripts of the Holy Books. Many devout believers refused to renounce the errors of their fathers, consecrated by tradition. Numerous rural settlements of *Raskolniki* (Schismatics), or *Starovery* (Old Believers), were subsequently established almost everywhere in Russia and, eventually, abroad. The dissenters did not want to base their faith on anything new except the old texts, despite the inaccuracies of the translation, done centuries ago, from Greek to Russian; and they would observe only old traditional customs and worship practices denounced by the present Russian Orthodox Church.

Eventually, persecution by the Russian tsarist government and aggressive treatment by their hostile neighbors and the State Orthodox Church forced Orthodox Old Believers into remote and undeveloped rural areas, where they quietly continued to practice their old rituals, periodically moving when threats of persecution by a hostile regime and intrusion by outsiders of different faiths and beliefs caught up with them again. Several of these groups migrated to the United States in the 1960s, settling in rural areas of Oregon and Alaska. Their obedience to pre-17th-century traditional worship practices places them in conspicuous contrast to, and often conflict with, other residents of their new locations. At the same time, elders complain that contact with a modern American culture is threatening the loyalty and discipline of their members, especially the younger ones. Despite tendencies toward acculturation and cultural change in some aspects of their present existence, Old Believers continue, to a large degree, to observe ancient traditions, worship practices and "living memory" in many cultural domains.

In the pages that follow, I provide a brief ethnohistoric overview of the people who became religious refugees and who have struggled for the past 350 years to maintain and protect their traditional and religious values. I describe the history of the Russian "Great Schism" (*Raskol*) of the 17th century and highlight essential elements of Russian Orthodox Old Believer ancient traditions and their current way of life in Alaska.

I have summarized the ethnographic descriptions contained in this book from research with Old Believers in Siberia conducted by Lyudmila P. Kuzmina; informal ethnographic observations and informal interviews that I conducted in Alaska in 1983, 1986, 1989, 1998, and 2001; informal interviews conducted by Miriam Lancaster in 1989; and secondary sources, reporting the results of research conducted in Oregon by Dr. Richard Morris (1981, 1982). Dr. Robert Muth (1985) collected macro-structural survey data on institutional structure as part of a broad study of structural-functional differentiation in Alaskan communities in 1984–85.

The first two editions of this title were published in 1991 and 1994 by the Alaska–Siberia Research Center (AKSRC) under the title *Change, Stability, and Values in the World of Culture. A Case from Russian Old Believers in Alaska.* The 3rd edition was published in 1998 by AKSRC under the title *Old Russia in Modern America: A Case from Russian Old Believers in Alaska.* The entire text of the book has been carefully revised and updated for this 4th edition, especially the chapter on the History of the "Great Schism" (*Raskol*) and sections on Religious Practices and Restrictions; Marriage, Marital Residence, Kinship, and Divorce; and Wedding Customs and Ceremonies.

I would like to express my thanks to Dr. Henry Michael (1913–2006), former Senior Fellow of the University Museum, University of Pennsylvania; Dr. Igor Kopytoff (1930–2013), Department of Anthropology, University of Pennsylvania; Professor *Emeritus* of Anthropology Wallace M. Olson (1932–2015), University of Alaska Southeast; Dr. Alexander Petrov, Institute of World History, Russian Academy of Sciences; and my assistant in field work, Miriam Lancaster, for useful comments and stimulating discussions of this research. Copy editors Dr. Linda Kruger, James Gebhardt, Dr. Ian Buvit, and proof reader Miriam Lancaster refined essential literary and technical aspects in the production of this edition. The board members and advisers of the Alaska–Siberia Research Center—Dr. Charles Holmes, Glenn Bacon, Mark Kissel, David McMahan, Maria Skuratovskaya, Jay Brodrick, and Peter Metcalfe—provided valuable comments and additional information. I also owe a debt of thanks to Dr. Ian Buvit for his support of this publication. I am especially grateful to the Old Believer communities in Alaska for their hospitality and for sharing the dramatic history and cultural traditions of their society with me.

Alexander B. Dolitsky
Alaska–Siberia Research Center

INTRODUCTION

Ethnic minorities, religious refugees, and other groups segregated by a dominant society have developed and implemented strategies and tactics intended to protect their national identity, religious practices, ancient traditions, and community cohesiveness. In most cases, the tactics and strategies of these unique orthodox groups, created to secure cultural continuity and "living memory" among their members, have historic roots and have resulted from cognitive rational choices.

The *Dukhobors*, members of a religious sect derived from Russian Orthodoxy in the 18th century, currently live in rural areas of Western Canada. In defending their values of practical religious communism, their members exercise pacifist strategies among their adherents and condemn those who violate them. The *Dukhobors'* pacifist "...tactics have helped to preserve them as a distinctive group and have delayed assimilation as long as the powerful trends toward social uniformity (which are deeper and less visible than those towards political uniformity) will allow" (Woodcock and Avakumovich 1968:12–13). [4]

Within the Hutterites, a Mennonite sect that originated in the 16th century in Europe, when social changes among their youth and a desire to assimilate with a dominant culture are detected, the elders tend to accept cultural innovations before the pressure for them becomes so great as to threaten the basic cohesiveness of the social system. They rewrite the rules of the society in accordance with new demands from members of their community. "Rules tend to be written down only when this common consensus starts to break down" (Eaton 1952:334). [5]

Historically, East European Jews lived in small cohesive villages in Russia, Belorussia, Poland, Ukraine, and other regions of Europe during the tsarist regime or prior to the October 1917 Socialist Revolution in Russia. The film *Fiddler on the Roof*, directed by Norman Jewison, quite accurately depicts the life of Jewish families in those villages—isolated

---

4   The *Dukhoborets*—a member of the Russian sect originating in the 18th century that emphasizes the supreme authority of inner experience and believes in the embodiment of the Spirit in different persons whom it follows as prophets and leaders, and that rejects all external ecclesiastical and civil authority to do military service or pay taxes. The *Dukhobors* have no church organization and hence no form of internal census. They neglect the Bible in favor of their own body of orally transmitted doctrine (Woodcock and Avakumovich 1968:1-25).

5   "The Hutterite religious practices began in Switzerland in 1528 and expended to form the contemporary Hutterite society in North America. Their forebears were severely persecuted by both Protestant and Catholic rulers. They were close to extermination several times. In 1770, a remnant of the sect found refuge and a promise of religious toleration in southern Russia. The Hutterites left Russia a little more than a century later to escape enforced Russification and military service" (Eaton 1952:332).

from urban centers, protective of their village boundaries and national traditions, obeying elders' and rabbis' advice for religious and secular matters, and following orthodox rules and traditions of Judaism. For centuries, their faith helped them survive as a nation, despite continuous hostility from their non-Jewish neighbors and oppressive governments. Today, modern Jewish families, mostly in Western urban societies, assimilate with dominant cultures at will, with the exception of certain Orthodox Jewish groups in a variety of locations. [6]

This process of assimilation, "...in which an individual has changed so much as to become dissociated from the value system of his group, or in which the entire group disappears as an autonomously functioning social system..." (Eaton 1952:339), is evident in today's many ethnic minority, religious refugee, and immigrant groups in the United States, including Alaska, and, presumably, in other free democratic societies around the world.

The history of the *Raskolniki* (Schismatics) or *Starovery* (Old Believers) is the most dramatic and vivid example of a large segment of people who opposed new liturgical and worship changes introduced in Russia by Patriarch Nikon in 1666-1667, and managed to preserve their 17th-century religious practices, national traditions, and core cultural values, despite constant exposure to various geographic, religious, ideological, economic, and social challenges to which they have been subjected for the past 350 years.

The central purpose of this book is to examine how much and how rapidly an isolated and traditional orthodox society may change its basic value systems or social integration within a dominant culture. In the pages that follow, I briefly summarize relevant aspects of Durkheimian evolutionary theory and concepts of social integration (Durkheim 1933 [1893], 1965 [1915]). Drawing on historical accounts and recent ethnographic and macro-structural research, I examine the persistence of Russian Orthodox Old Believer culture in light of this theoretical perspective. I posit that the cultural persistence evidenced by Old Believer settlements is due to the cognitive rational preselection and/or rejection of culture traits and adaptive strategies (Boehm 1968, Bennett 1969, 1976, Dolitsky and Plaskett 1985) that have demonstrated their survival value, cultural continuity, and "living memory" during lengthy periods of religious persecution and geographical relocations.

This theoretical perspective is presented and supported using ethnographic data obtained from Russian Old Believer communities that, for the most part, still preserve their traditional style of life in Siberia and North America. This book is not intended as a detailed and spatial analysis of Old Believer society, nor

---

6   Almost 2,000 years ago, many Jews were forced to leave their homeland in Palestine. This diaspora sent Jews to different parts of the world. Wherever Jews settled, they maintained their identity as a people by living in close-knit and cohesive communities and obeying their religious laws and traditions. These traditions set Jews apart from outsiders; yet, these traditions also helped them survive centuries of persecution and antisemitism.

as a comparative analysis of Old Believers with other isolated and conservative traditional communities. Rather, it is a brief ethnohistoric overview of the people who, by historic circumstances, were forced to become religious refugees and, as a result, were determined to protect their traditional and religious values and lifestyle.

This book leaves a number of questions unanswered and recommends them for further research to help us better understand Russian Old Believer social structure: Why do Old Believers today do what they do? What social control mechanisms do these communities have to enforce conformity and cohesiveness? How does their inclusion in a capitalistic, cash-based economy affect their social organization and culture? How do they reconcile differing historic and regional practices within a given community? What strategies and tactics do Old Believers in Alaska use to protect and maintain their ancient traditions and core cultural values? How do Old Believers control their acculturation and possible assimilation within a dominant society?

Alexander B. Dolitsky
Alaska–Siberia Research Center

SOCIO-CULTURAL EVOLUTION:
A THEORETICAL PERSPECTIVE OF CULTURE CHANGE

The chief concerns of the social sciences, and of ethnohistory in particular, are the study of culture change and culture processes in diachronic and synchronic terms (Steward 1955, Sturtevant 1966, Helms 1978, Axtell 1979), and the reconstruction of ethnogenetic processes and ethnic history of the different peoples of the world, including their blood and cultural relationships (Bromley 1979, 1983, Gurvich 1980, 1982).[1]

The question of culture change and stability is complex. Culture change is the process by which some members of a society revise their cultural knowledge and social acceptance, performance, and integration processes. Briefly, culture change means a revision of the knowledge used to generate social behavior (Spradley and McCurdy 1975). In order for culture change to occur, individuals must revise their present knowledge and create new ways of interpreting and understanding experience. More than the mere learning of new information, culture change involves the adoption of new forms of social behavior. Only when new information is used to interpret experience and generate new behavior does it become cultural knowledge. Often, though, people may have access to new information and they either fail to grasp its meaning, refuse to believe its content, or are unable to use this knowledge to reorganize their behavior. Sometimes new information conflicts with deeply held values, and even though people acquire new knowledge, they may not change their traditional and other-worldly cultural patterns.

Isolated communities and segregated religiously oriented groups are largely static (Eaton 1952, Hostetler 1965, Dolitsky and Kuzmina 1986, Scheffel 1989). Despite occasional changes brought about by technological inventions and/or exploration of new territories, stable and conservative traditions are transmitted with little modification from generation to generation. Religiously oriented Amish farmers in North America, for example, have remained mostly unmechanized and virtually self-sufficient for the past 250 years, while in rural America, in general, there has been a tendency to accept and use technological changes and inventions (Hostetler 1965:11).[2] The Hutterite society in North America has been described as "...an island of certainty and security in a river of change, ...an unspoiled rural Utopia" (Eaton 1952:332).

---

1   The search for ethnogenetic relationships is the central research objective of the former Soviet and Russian historical discipline and it comes into play in determining cultural areas and their spatio-temporal relationships. In short, the term *ethnogenesis* simply means a historical continuity or transformation of one cultural tradition into another in an attempt to discover the traits found in certain ethnic traditions and the historical origins of these traits (Dolgikh 1964, Dolitsky 1984, 1985, 1990).

2   Swiss Mennonite bishop (1693), the founder of the sect of Mennonite followers of Amman that settled in North America.

Some anthropological theorists, however, contend that the model of cultural stability of isolated societies is both artificial and erroneous. Keesing (1963:386) argues that "models of the dynamics of the completely self-contained culture and societies are necessarily inferential. No scientist can observe a completely isolated group in the contemporary world—he would not be there, or written records would not be kept, if it were so."

In dealing with cultural phenomena such as stability or acculturation, it becomes obvious that the value systems of the culture concerned (i.e., individual and group judgments of the worth of new and old elements as expressed in effectively charged choices) are the key to understanding short- and long-term social evolution and adaptive behavior (Wallis 1952, Frake 1962, Bennett 1969, 1976). Specifically, "...the members of the conservative groups make their decisions not merely with regard to the present carriers of the culture, but rather for the next generation in perspective" (Wallis 1952:146). In other words, cultural value systems, "...as a heterogeneous class of normative factors" (Albert 1956:221), have a screening effect on stability and change and are central to understanding cultural processes.

The evolutionary perspective is one theoretical approach brought forth to interpret the process of culture change. In the study of culture change and stability, few themes in the social science literature have received greater attention than the debate over cultural evolution. This topic has been addressed by many prominent thinkers and theoreticians, including Tylor (1958 [1871]), Morgan (1963 [1877]), Durkheim (1933 [1893]), White (1945, 1949, 1959), Steward (1955, 1956), Sahlins and Service (1960), Parsons (1964, 1966), Harris (1968, 1974), Nisbet (1969, 1970), Eisenstadt (1964, 1970, 2004), Sahlins (1977), Kurland and Beckerman (1985), and Rindos (1985).

Since it arose in the late 19th century, the evolutionary perspective has experienced alternating periods of preeminence and disruption. Those who have adopted the 19th-century evolutionary perspective espouse the view that societies evolve through stages of gradual step-by-step cultural development from a simple level of social development to more complex levels. Through the cumulative addition of culture traits, societies evolve from the simple to the complex by means of the progressive differentiation of social functions. "That society is the most evolved which has the highest degree of functional differentiation, whether in the form of occupational specialization or organizational complexity" (Naroll 1956:687).

Opponents of unilinear evolutionary theory, on the other hand, believe either that no such developmental sequence exists as an historical fact (Nisbet 1970), or that laws of evolutionary change are too complex to be determined (Boas 1932, 1938). Boas recommended a return to factual evidence and to what came to be called "historical particularism" (Harris 1968). Briefly, cultural historical interpretation is based on an inductive research methodology and normative view of culture. Within this framework, the cultural historical approach emphasizes synthesis based upon the chronological and special ordering of historical data. From this perspective, the synthesis is directed toward outlining the sequence and geographical distribution of past events. Though a salutary reaction, it nevertheless was carried too far. "The loss of evolutionary mode of thought also meant loss of general problem orientation. Problems, such as they were, remained specifically historical. More general questions of development, function, and process were left alone" (Willey and Sabloff 1974:81).

At the present time, the evolutionary perspective on culture change has a number of adherents in both anthropology and sociology. With the development of techniques of scalogram analysis, interest in discovering evolutionary sequences of cultural and institutional development has been renewed (Naroll 1956, Freeman and Winch 1957, Carneiro 1962, Carneiro and Tobias 1963, Young and Young 1973). In issuing a call for an additional look at the process of cultural evolution, Robert Carneiro (1962:159), for instance, has suggested that efforts toward discovering an evolutionary sequence that most societies have followed "…were hindered in the past by the belief that it was more noble to discover the exception which refuted a universal sequence than it was to construct a sequence to which a preponderant number of cases adhered." While there is much to be learned from this approach, studying exceptions often may be just as illuminating as searching for universals. When situations emerge as exceptions to the tenets of a dominant explanatory paradigm, they warrant further research. The Hutterite communities in North America, Russian Orthodox Old Believers in various countries of the world, including Alaska, *Dukhobors* in Canada and Amish settlements in the United States are examples of sub-systems, which have not followed the developmental sequence of their enveloping culture systems (Eaton 1952, Hostetler 1965, Dolitsky and Kuzmina 1986, Dolitsky 1994, 1998, 2007, 2009).

DURKHEIM'S THEORY OF SOCIO-CULTURAL EVOLUTION

David Émile Durkheim (1858–1917) was a prominent French sociologist, social psychologist and philosopher. He formally established the academic discipline of sociology and is commonly known as the principal architect of modern social science. Much of Durkheim's work focused on how societies could maintain their integrity and coherence in modernity; an era in which new social institutions and major theoretical perspectives in the social sciences have come into being. "One of its central postulates was that early societies, and also 'primitives,' were dominated by a kind of collectivity of mental processes often spoken of as *the group mind*...[or]...as the 'collective representations' of the group..." (Keesing 1963:176).

Durkheim viewed the evolution of socio-cultural development as an inexorable, unilinear process. To Durkheim, social evolution was the process whereby societies evolve through six developmental stages, beginning with (1) the horde, and progressing through (2) the tribe, composed of clans, (3) the tribal confederation, (4) the ancient city-state, (5) medieval society, and finally, (6) the modern industrial state (Durkheim 1933 [1893], Wallwork 1984). Referred to by Durkheim as the division of social labor, this process is characterized by increasing differentiation of social structure — a process in which economic, educational, political, legal, and other social functions become gradually disembodied from the institutions of religion and kinship and incorporated into social structure as autonomous units. Although Durkheim acknowledged that structural specialization could manifest itself in different cultural forms in various societies, he argued that the process of structural differentiation was an evolutionary imperative through which societies must pass in their transformation from egalitarian social forms into more complex ones.

Durkheim attributed the cause of structural differentiation to the increasing physical and moral density of human beings in those societies experiencing pressures due to increasing population and technological changes in communication and transportation. According to Durkheim, an increase in physical density was a necessary condition to give rise to structural differentiation. Increases in physical density must be accompanied by increases in moral density; and increases in moral density are greatly facilitated by development of transportation and communication networks, and by concentration of populations through constructive geographic boundaries and political centralization. Durkheim cited 19th-century Russia and China as examples of societies characterized by high physical (but not moral) density, and, thus, a low level of structural differentiation. As people came into closer and more frequent contact, competition ensued among individual members of society for available social roles and resources. As competitive pressures become more acute, the less adaptive members of society face two alternatives: differentiation into more specialized functional niches, or, in Durkheim's word, elimination.[3]

For Durkheim, it was obvious that of the alternative responses to increased competitiveness resulting from physical and moral density, structural differentiation provides the key to normative social integration. Through the division of labor, individuals who occupy increasingly specialized roles and functions are bound to each other and to society through the need to cooperate with one another. Individual members of egalitarian, less-differentiated societies are held together through the "mechanical solidarity" engendered by collective representations and similar or common values. But as structural differentiation progresses, individual units become bound to society by means of "organic solidarity," that is, through their increasing functional interdependence (Durkheim 1933 [1893]).

Durkheim was heavily influenced by the Darwinian paradigm of evolution, which was sweeping the Western scientific world during the last half of the 19th century. As Turner (1981:381) has observed: "…almost all of Durkheim's major insights are expressed within an evolutionary, causal, and functional mode of reasoning." Nowhere is this more apparent than in *The Division of Labor in Society*, where Durkheim discusses the progress of structural differentiation in terms of an inexorable evolutionary process, moving forward from relatively "primitive" conditions to more complex ones.

---

3 Durkheim was uncharacteristically vague concerning the disposition of unsuccessful competitors in the struggle for existence. In *The Division of Labor in Society*, he acknowledges such potential solutions as: "…emigration, colonization, resignation to a precarious, disputed existence, and finally, the total elimination of the weakest by suicide or some other means" (Durkheim 1933:286). A number of other possibilities exist, however, in the struggle for existence. In a perceptive review of Durkheimian theory, for example, Schnore (1958:626) states: "It [intensification of competition] might lead simply to the elimination by natural selection of a larger proportion of those born." Albert (1956:221–48) extends the list of alternatives: "…of course, there are many other ways out, such as migration, suicide, civil war, crime, etc."

POST-DURKHEIMIAN DEVELOPMENTS
IN EVOLUTIONARY THEORY

Émile Durkheim's theory of evolution has been the subject of considerable analytical review. Work by post-Durkheimian theorists and applied scientists has served both to reaffirm substantial portions of his theoretical position, while, at the same time, to extend his theory into a more comprehensive reformation. Although a comprehensive review of evolutionary theory since Durkheim is beyond the scope of this book, I would like to discuss a number of relevant conceptual refinements of the Durkheimian paradigm which bear on the description of cultural persistence and change in Old Believer settlements in modern Alaska that follows.

Durkheim's unilinear view of evolution, as well as his criteria of structural-functional differentiation, has been the subject of critical attention from a number of social theorists with the advantage of over half a century of hindsight (Malinowski 1931, Merton 1934, Sahlins and Service 1960, Eisenstadt 1970, Steward 1976, Wallwork 1984). Steward (1955, 1976), for example, formulated a multilinear theory of cultural evolution. His major criticism of unilinear evolutionists, Leslie White (1949) in particular, was that they operated on a very broad and general level of analysis. More interested in specific cultures rather than with a culture as a unified whole, Steward formulated his ecological approach in order to explain the relationship between people and the environment: how people incorporate nature and society, and what they do to themselves, nature, and society in the process. Steward (1955) emphasized the role of the biophysical environment as a causal factor in the development and adoption of social institutions. His cultural-ecological approach attempts to define the relationship among natural resources, subsistence technology, and the behavior required to bring technology to bear upon resources. Steward succeeds in demonstrating functional relationships but does not establish causality of human strategic and rational behavior.

Eisenstadt (1970), drawing on the results of a growing proliferation of modernization studies, states that theories of socio-cultural evolution require reappraisal. Through the judicious use of historical examples from his study of empires, he demonstrates that different institutional spheres (e.g., political, religious, economic) within the same society increase and/or decrease in complexity at much different rates; there is no reason to believe that they all will reach similar stages of socio-cultural complexity, or that their social structures will take on the same institutional contours, even if they attain similar socio-economic stages (Eisenstadt 1964, 1970). "The search for universal causes of change or for one 'central' 'basic cause', the polemics as to whether such change is exogenous to a social system or inherent in it, the controversy concerning 'static' and 'dynamic' sociology, have all greatly contributed to this lack of agreement"(Eisenstadt 1970:3).

Thus, certain post-Durkheimian theorists perceive evolutionary culture change as far from being a phenomenon which marches ever-forward through a series of unilinear sequential stages. Rather, it is best characterized as occurring in fits and starts, subject to regression, stagnation, breakdown, and retrenchment. In other words, forces of persistence, stability, and dedifferentiation co-exist along with the impetus toward evolution (Muth 1985).

In spite of these criticisms, the view that socio-cultural evolution is a unilineal process has continued to prevail among Russian social scientists (Bromley 1983, Bromley and Markova 1982, Gurvich 1980, 1982, Derevyanko et al. 1989, Moscalenko and Okladnikov 1983) and many Western scholars (White 1945, Radcliffe-Brown 1952, Naroll 1956, Freeman and Winch 1957, Carneiro 1962, 1967, Carneiro and Tobias 1963, Lenski 1966, Parsons 1966, 1971, Young and Young 1973). Until dissolution of the Soviet Union and other socialist countries in the early 1990s, Russian and East European social scientists subscribed to a traditional view of the dialectical and historical materialist philosophy, arguing that physical environment is a major factor in the biological evolution of humans, and technology, i.e., mode of production in the specific socio-economic stages, is a main cause of cultural change in societies (Bromley 1983, Ilichev 1982, Moscalenko and Okladnikov 1983). Bromley (1983) states that the development of ethnic traditions must incorporate three major categories: physical environment, social factors, and ethnic factors. In sum, most Russian social scientists argued that under the same or similar environmental conditions, socio-economic stages, and objective and subjective historical circumstances, the social outcome of given societies would be alike; thus, one should study cultures and societies by applying general laws of dialectical and historical materialism and by treating them as a unified whole (Bromley and Markova 1982, Ilichev 1982, Moscalenko and Okladnikov 1983).

Meanwhile, during the last five decades in the United States, a number of scholars in both sociology and anthropology have applied techniques of scalogram analysis to the study of socio-cultural evolution. Their results have led them to conclude that social systems progress through evolutionary sequences of socio-cultural development. Initial attempts to empirically identify a sequence of evolutionary development were undertaken by Naroll (1956) in anthropology and Freeman and Winch (1957) in sociology. Robert Carneiro (1962, 1963, 1967) developed subsequent applications of scalogram analysis to cultural evolution. Carneiro was able to rank-order 100 societies according to their cultural complexity. His work led him to conclude that many anthropologists in the United States rejected the idea of unilinear evolution too readily and too completely:

> *The idea of a main sequence of cultural development is closely akin to the familiar notion of unilinear evolution. According to both, there is a discernible order to the way in which societies develop, and this order is substantially duplicated by all societies if and as they evolve. But there*

is also a difference: instead of saying that societies tend to go through the same stages, we should say that societies tend to evolve traits in the same order.

At the same time that traits are rank-ordered into a main sequence of evolution, societies are rank-ordered in terms of their complexity or degree of development. Thus, scale analysis provides one way of placing cultures along an evolutionary continuum (Carneiro and Tobias 1963:203).

Robert Carneiro deliberately applied the Guttman scaling technique to a Durkheimian level of analysis, as he studied cultures and societies as a whole.[4] In sociology, meanwhile, Frank Young and his colleagues were applying scalogram techniques to the institutional components of community-level social systems (Young and Young 1973). Through the use of a technique known as a macro-structural survey, Young and his students demonstrated that the institutional structures of communities within a regional system differentiated in a pattern predictable by applying Guttman scalogram analysis (Young and Fujimoto 1965, Spencer 1967, Young and Young 1973). The replicability of his results led Young to conclude that communities within a relatively similar regional system "grow" and accumulate culture traits or institutions in a cumulative, unilinear, evolutionary sequence (Muth 1985).

As I have attempted to demonstrate through this brief discussion, the evolutionary perspective of socio-cultural change continues to be popular in modern anthropology and sociology. Although it is not without its critics, there are both theorists and applied scientists within the social sciences who think that the evolutionary theory adequately (but not perfectly) explains the empirical reality of socio-cultural change.

What are we to make of it, then, when a situation arises that appears to contradict the constructs of a prevailing theoretical paradigm? Such is the case with the culture of Russian Old Believers. Since the mid-17th century, the core cultural values and ancient Orthodox institutions of Old Believers have changed very little, despite exposure to a multitude of different socio-physical environments over the course of 350 years. In this book, I offer my interpretation of the culture change and persistence of the Russian Old Believer community in Alaska within the context of Durkheimian evolutionary theory and framework.

---

4   Guttman scaling is also referred to as cumulative scaling or scalogram analysis. The purpose of Guttman scaling is to establish a one-dimensional continuum for a concept one wishes to measure.

HISTORY OF THE "GREAT SCHISM" (*RASKOL*)

The Mongolian domination, the shift of Russian statehood northward, and isolation of the Russian Orthodox Church from Byzantine theology, led to a decline of learning, which resulted in many errors and discrepancies in translating the Holy Texts from Greek into *Church Slavonic*. As early as the mid-16th century, attempts were made to correct the errors in order to attain conformity in rituals. Only in the mid-17th century (1652–66), however, were the Russian Orthodox Church and all of Russia shaken to the core by what has since been called the "Great Schism" *(Raskol)*. At the time, Nikon (1605-1681), a strong-minded patriarch, scholar and strict disciplinarian, wanted to correct the Holy Texts by introducing changes in the church books and the method of worship practiced by the Russian masses since the inception of Christianity in Russia in the 10th century. These changes dealt with revising the church books, where errors, marginal notes, and mistranslations had become incorporated into the texts over time. His corrections also included changes in rituals, revising several of the actions that the faithful and illiterate peasants had internalized as part of the mystical context of their worship.

Nikon demanded that Russian practices conform at every point to the standard of the four ancient patriarchates, and that the Russian service books be altered wherever they differed from the Greek. In 1653, Nikon sent a memorandum to churches across the land, instructing them in various revisions of the services and the books. Among major points of contention were: (1) how many fingers would be used to make the sign of the cross — two or three, (2) the spelling of Jesus' name, (3) whether "Alleluia" should be sung two or three times, (4) the retention of certain words and phrases in the Creed, (5) the number of hosts to be used in the liturgy, and (6) whether the priests should walk around the altar with or against the passage of the sun (Grunwald 1962:154). This policy was aimed at those who regarded Moscow as the Third Rome and Russia as the stronghold and norm of Orthodoxy. By establishing Greek practices in Russia, Nikon also pursued a second goal: to make the church supreme over the state. "The Russians certainly respected the memory of the Mother Church of Byzantium from which they had received the faith, but they did not feel the same reverence for contemporary Greeks" (Ware 1986:121).

This may seem a trivial matter, but in the eyes of simple believers a change in a symbol constituted a change in the faith. Members of the Russian opposition to Nikon's reforms insisted that: (1) the sign of the cross should be made with two outstretched fingers (*dvoyeperstiye*) rather than with three fingers held together (*troyeperstiye*),[5] (2) the quadrupling of "Alleluia" singing in the doxology — the

---

5 The conservatives maintained that the sign of the cross with two fingers rather than three (the latter being the proposed reform) signified the dual nature of Christ, with the first finger representing the divine nature and the bent second being a symbol of Christ's descent to Earth for the salvation of humankind. They cited many old icons to support their position on this matter, in which some of the saints and Christ could be seen using the two-

praise of the Lord — should be chanted twice and not three times; (3) the name Jesus *(Isus)* should be spelled and pronounced with one 'I' rather than two 'Is' *(Iisus)*; (4) processions around the church should move clockwise rather than counter-clockwise; (5) crosses on churches and tombs must have eight ends rather than six or four; (6) in accordance with 'the doctrine of the trees,' crosses on churches must be made of certain types of timber only; (7) rosaries should be used in prayer also by laymen, and that such rosaries must be made of leather; and (8) seven rather than five hosts should be used in the Eucharist (Gerschenkron 1970).

Pre-reform matters of ritual were the embodiment of certain theological precepts and ideological alliances, and hence stirred considerable controversy upon their arrival. Changes proposed by the Patriarch Nikon became the focus of opposition for those who held onto the old ritual, the old belief. Labeled *Raskolniki* (people of the schism) by the reformers, they called themselves Old Believers *(Starovery)* or True Believers (it would be more exact to call them Old Ritualists or *Staroobryadtsy*). Old Believers stubbornly pointed out that they were not splitting away from the church, but that the reformers were drawing the church away from the true Orthodox rituals. No doctrinal point, however, reflecting a perceptible difference in the conception of the world was involved in the schism.

For the Russian masses, the organized religion of the Orthodox Church was interwoven with superstition and confused with magic. Many stubbornly opposed the changes in rituals simply because Nikon promoted them, but many others refused to conform to them, strongly questioning the authority of the patriarch to make such alterations. After all, the Orthodox Church, with the purity of its apostolic succession traced to St. Andrew, had protected itself from the "Roman Heresy" and had steadfastly remained untainted while Constantinople, the capital of Byzantium, or the "Second Rome," fell into the hands of the Turks in 1453. While Moscow increased its power, independence, self-esteem and territories, in particular the acquisition of Kiev in 1667, many favored the concept of Moscow as the "Third Rome." Having preserved its purity, while the others had lost theirs, Russian Orthodoxy was believed by the Russians to be the only remaining survivor of the true church and they counseled a deliberate withdrawal from Greek tutelage. Given these considerations, how could Patriarch Nikon dare to order changes? Opposition to the innovations was also tied to an important psychological factor: the traditional forms and familiar routines gave an illusion of security. The people, insecure amid chronic religious disorders, bitterly opposed new and further efforts to uproot the old rituals (Zenkovsky 1957, Klyuchevsky 1960 [1913], Vernadsky 1969, Soloviev 1980).

Old Believers thought that the Russian state was of the Antichrist and that the end of the world was at hand. Old Believers of all factions and branches also believed that the Antichrist's evil spirit was at work through Nikon, and

---

fingered sign. The three-fingered sign was intended as an acknowledgment of the Holy Trinity. But this was considered by the conservative dissenters to represent Greek heresy.

the Tsar Alexis himself was the Antichrist. "Many of its adherents encapsulated their hatred of everything new and oppressive in Russian life in the apocalyptic symbol of the Antichrist. The symbol and the mood it expressed demanded resistance to the state and the official church — the instruments of the Antichrist. For, in both symbolic and practical terms, the faithful were not to submit to his power" (Crummey 1970:219).

Though the schism was basically a religious phenomenon, it also involved broader socio-political factors. In order to understand this historical event and its circumstances, one must realize that the church was not an isolated institution within the state, but part of the ideological norms and values of 17th-century Russia (Pokrovsky 1933, Zenkovsky 1957). Two distinct classes of clergy in the Russian Orthodox Church controlled social and political attitudes within the state. The parish priests, known as the *white clergy* because of the white garments they wore, represented the interests of the common people and peasants in many ways. They served two masters — the village commune that selected and paid them and limited their actions, and the higher ecclesiastics by whom they were taxed. The higher clergy, called the *black clergy*, were all monks. They were the servants of the tsar, and, just as members of the *white clergy*, were the servants of the villages. No member of the *white clergy* could hope for promotion to the places of power and wealth, such as the bishoprics and archbishoprics, since these were the monopoly of the *black clergy*.

Between the *black* and the *white clergies* existed an almost unbridgeable gap and constant controversies. Rebellions against the authority of the higher churchmen were frequent, and there was persistent opposition on the part of the lower (*white*) clergy toward efforts to increase and centralize clerical authority. These efforts climaxed during the Patriarchate of Nikon (1652–58), who sought to reform and revitalize the church. In fact, he was not the first to attempt to adopt changes in the Russian Church, nor did his efforts initially arouse opposition. But his attempts at reform became the immediate cause of the "Great Schism" (*Raskol*), partly because he had many personal enemies who were glad to use the controversy as an opportunity to eliminate Nikon from the center of Church authority. In 1658, Nikon withdrew into semi-retirement but did not resign the office of Patriarch. For eight years, the Russian Church remained without an effective head, until, at Tsar Alexis's request, a great Council was held in Moscow between 1666-1667 over which the patriarchs of Alexandria and Antioch presided (Ware 1986:125).

The specific opposition to Nikon's reform was at first confined to the higher (*black*) clergy, but under the leadership of Nikita Dobrynin and Archpriest Avvakum, the movement spread widely to the streets of Moscow and beyond. "Avvakum and his followers regarded the tiny changes in spelling suggested by Nikon as a cardinal criterion of Christianity as such, and a portent of the coming of the Antichrist" (Carmichael 1968:77, Crummey 1970).

By mobilizing the Russian population against the church and against Nikon, the early Old Believers helped lay the intellectual foundations of Old Belief and could, therefore, hardly be pardoned by the church. Clearly, the Old Believers had a large following, which included both ordinary laymen and prominent members of the local church hierarchy (Michels 1997). As a result of the popular rebellion against the church, Patriarch Nikon lost the favor of Tsar Alexis and his enemies removed him from control of the church, but the quarrel raged on between those who supported the changes and those who opposed them. Finally, the Church Council called in 1666–1667 decided in favor of Nikon's reforms, but against him. Violence began almost at once and was marked by monstrous cruelties for four decades. Nikon's changes in the service books and above all his ruling on the sign of the Cross were confirmed, but Nikon himself was deposed and exiled; a new patriarch was appointed in his place. The Council was, therefore, a triumph for Nikon's policy of imposing Greek practices on the Russian Orthodox Church, but a defeat for his attempt to set the patriarch above the tsar (Ware 1986:125).

Tsar Alexis was on the side of the reformers and eventually approved the reforms, making refusal to conform not just an offense against the church, but a civil offense as well; the tsar began to openly wage campaigns against the conservatives. Tsarist approval of the church reforms involved political motivations, such as national independence from the Byzantium and Greek Orthodoxy influence, governmental control of the ideological institutions, the long process of territorial growth of the Russian state, particularly the expansion southward, and continuing efforts of political and economic centralization of Russian lands under the Moscow authorities.

The schism and purge also weakened the church and later made it easier for Peter the Great (1672–1725) to subordinate it in order to strengthen his autocracy and enforce new socio-political reforms in Russia (Kluchevsky 1913, Pokrovsky 1933). Peter the Great identified himself with the official church by placing it under the rule of the absolutist state. In 1721, the tsar abolished the patriarchate as well as the church council and assumed the position as supreme head of the church through control of a chief procurator called "The Tsar's Eye." The abolition of the patriarchate was part of a wider process: Peter sought not only to deprive the church of leadership, but also to eliminate it from any participation in social and government work.

Because the power of the tsar stood behind the Church Council of 1666–1667, the schismatics were in fact rebels against both church and state. To oppose imminent unrest among Russian masses, the government searched for and punished the most active rebels of the movement. Archpriest Avvakum, the most instrumental and effective leader of the Old Believers, was burned at the stake in 1682 after having been exiled for 10 years and imprisoned for 22 years. From then on, the decree of 1685, issued by the Regent Sophia, sanctioned burning at the stake and jailing or exiling those who preached old beliefs and refused to repent after thrice repeated torture. In protest, whole communities of Old Believers often would lock themselves in their wooden chapels and set them on fire, preferring self-inflicted death (Stepniak 1977 [1888], Ware 1986). [6]

A prominent Russian historian of the 19th century Nikolay Kostomarov (1817–1885) preserved a graphic account of a case which manifests how and why the *Raskol* became so contentious:

> *It was in Tumen, a town in Western Siberia; time, Sunday morning. The priests were celebrating the mass in the cathedral on the lines of the new missals, as usual. The congregation was listening calmly to the service, when, at the moment of the solemn appearance of the consecrated water, a female voice shouted, "Orthodox! Do not bow! They carry a dead body; the water is stamped with the unholy cross, the seal of Antichrist."*
>
> *The speaker was a female Raskolnik, accompanied by a male coreligionist of hers, who thus interrupted the service. The man and woman were seized, knouted in the public square, and thrown into prison. But their act produced its effect. When another Raskolnik, the monk Danilo, shortly after appeared on the same spot and began to preach, an excited crowd at once gathered around him. His words affected his audience so deeply that girls and old women began to see the skies open above them, and the Virgin Mary, with the angels, holding a crown of glory over those who refused to pray as they were ordered by the authorities. Danilo persuaded them to flee into the wilderness for the sake of the true faith. Three hundred people, both men and women, joined him, but a strong body of armed men was sent in pursuit. They could not escape, and Danilo seized the moment to preach to them, and persuade them that the hour had come for all of them to receive "the baptism of fire." By this he meant they were to burn themselves alive. They accordingly locked themselves up in a big wooden shed, set fire to it, and perished in the flames—all the three hundred, with their leader* (cited from Stepniak 1977:256–57 [1888]).

Another graphic account of Old Believer opposition to the authority of the official church and state by means of collective self-mutilation was described by French historian and biographer Henri Troyat (1991:26):

> *Some sectarians slept in coffins, others flagellated each other, still others condemned themselves to eternal silence, castrated themselves, cut one another's throats, or locked themselves up in a house with their families, set fire to piles of straw, and perished in the flames singing hymns*

---

6 It has been estimated that during the two decades between 1672–91 some 20,000 people burned themselves to death to protest new changes in worship. Whole groups, sometimes as many as 2,500 at a time, would pack themselves into huts and set the structure on fire (Carmichael 1968:77).

to be sure of entering paradise. Under pressure from their fanatical parents, children would say: "We will go to the stake; in the other world we will have little red boots and shirts embroidered with gold thread; they will give us all the honey, nuts, and apples we want; we will not bow down before the Antichrist." Soldiers were sent to prevent these autos-da-fe [ritual of public penance]. *But their arrival only precipitated the madness of the fanatics, who would throw themselves by hundreds into the purifying flames. The most reasonable of the schismatics sought refuge in the forests, organized themselves into autonomous communities, and lived soberly by their labor, refusing the aid of the priests and professing among themselves the faith of the ancestors. Thus, Russians' heresy included a whole psychological spectrum, from demented excesses of some to the quiet protest of others.*

Although many were purged, the movement to preserve Old Orthodox rituals still persisted. From this polarization evolved large segments of those who risked persecution, exile or death rather than give up the old rituals and traditions. As the government embarked upon the repression, most rebels, families and groups began to flee from the major population areas of the Russian State.

Their protest was soon to be eclipsed by other problems that beset the growing and developing Russian nation state. As Russia lumbered through its wars and social strife, the Old Believers took refuge in undeveloped areas of the country, thereby avoiding persecution for their continued lack of obedience to the tsar's commands. Periodic reprieves and attempts to re-incorporate these people as *yedinovertsy* (monobelievers) met with only moderate success. Thus, Old Believers or *Starovery*, came to represent the groups that rejected the church reforms of 17th-century Russia and found themselves in opposition to the established Orthodox Church and Russian tsarist authorities.

WORLD-WIDE MIGRATION OF RUSSIAN OLD BELIEVERS

Within a few decades of the schism, many Old Believers escaped Russia to densely wooded areas of Belorussia and northern Ukraine, southward to the Don and Kuban rivers, northward toward the Baltic Sea and Arctic shores and, beyond the boundaries of the state, to neighboring Romania, Turkey, and Poland (Vetka region). Others settled in southern Siberia (Altay Mountains), the Far East, and Central Asia (Figure 1). Through the centuries, these remote groups, not necessarily in contact with each other, and, in spite of minimal levels of modernization, acculturation, and adaptation to new climates, not only survived but also preserved and maintained their religious form of worship and their cultural ways.

All of the Old Believer groups that settled east of Lake Baykal, for example, in the 17th and 18th centuries maintained contact with the Buryats, Evenks, and other neighboring ethnic groups who were engaged in hunting, reindeer breeding, fishing, and raising sled dogs. Trans-Baykalian Old Believers, whose ancestors were banished to eastern Siberia from the Chernigov Province of Ukraine and Vetka of Poland in the 18th century, moved with their families and are known, therefore, as *semeyskiye* (of the family)—from the Russian word *semya* (family). The Russian newcomers found themselves in conditions radically different from their customary life. Long winters, bitter frosts, harsh physical and social environment, and a shortage of Russian women—all these necessitated urgent acculturation in line with the centuries-old experience of the aboriginal population in economic activities and in coping with the severe natural conditions. Although Old Believers of the Trans-Baykal fanatically followed the patriarchal traditions of the pre-reform Russian Orthodox Church, their members, including women, were better educated than their neighbors. Many of them were *kuptsy* (traders), *kazaks* (free peasants and border guards), *remeslenniki* (craftsmen), or farmers (Bromley and Markova 1982:235).

In the 1980s, about 100,000 Russian Old Believers lived in the area east of Lake Baykal (Kuzmina 1982). The small villages of the early settlers of the 19th century have become large communities, with modern houses in a traditional architectural style and streets a few kilometers long. According to Kuzmina (1982, 1983), the settlements show that many conservative forms of life and religious practices are gradually subsiding into the past, together with such norms of the everyday life as the prohibition of any communication with representatives of other faiths, to say nothing of inter-religious marriages, and the banning of wine and tea drinking, smoking, and beard shaving. However, the Trans-Baykal Old Believers continue to live and work in compact groups, and they try to preserve their traditional customs by marrying within their own community or converting an outsider to their religion and traditional ways of life. In contrast to other Russian groups, they rarely come into economic (e.g., trade, exchange of goods and services, business contracts) or other social contact with native Buryats. Despite considerable transformations in the culture of contemporary villages, the Old Believers of Trans-Baykal still maintain many aspects of their cultural traditions of the pre-reform 17th-century Russia. A manifestation of these architectural features can be seen in the layout of their modern villages. The traditional-style houses, decorations, and exterior paintings remind one of the feudal farmsteads of the nobility described in Old-Russian chronicles and folk tales (Figure 2). The maintenance of their tradition can also be seen in the brightly colored women's clothes, consisting of multi-colored *sarafans* (variations of skirts) and jackets of unusual cuts, headwear that shares many traits with the appearance of 17th- and 18th-century Russian women (Figure 3). Traditional singing, based on a great number of rhythmically complex voice parts, is reflected in the repertoire of the choir *Kunaleya* from the *semeyskiy* village *Bolshoy Kunaley* of Trans-Baykal (Eliasov 1963, Dorofeev 1980, Kuzmina 1982, 1983).

In assessing the cultural traditions of Old Believers, one should not neglect its contemporary state among that part of the Trans-Baykalian Old Believer community, who moved to Manchuria during the construction of the East Chinese Railroad and the city of Kharbin. They subsequently gave rise to the Old Believer community of *Kharbinskaya*; residents are called *Kharbintsy*. After the Socialist October Revolution in 1917, Russian Old Believers faced the atheistic Soviet government bent on discouraging, but reluctantly tolerating, all forms of religion. During the 1920s, in desperation, many of the Siberian Old Believers escaped over the border to China, where they once again lived in isolated and remote areas of Manchuria, in the city of Kharbin[7] and the Sinkiang region[8] (Figure 1).

As a result of the Chinese Communist Revolution of 1949, many of them were moved onto collective farms, provided a meager food allowance, and given mandatory work requirements. Many, eventually, were sent back to the Soviet Union. Finally, after 10 years, a minority of them, as families, groups,

---

7   There are few reliable estimates of how many Russians fled to exile in northern China during this period. One such estimate suggests that the population of the city of Kharbin during 1933 was more than a quarter Russian, with the total number of people in the city being 384,570 (Dr. Igor Kopytoff, personal communication in 1998 and 2000. Dr. Kopytoff (1930–2013), Professor *Emeritus* of Anthropology at the University of Pennsylvania, was born in Manchuria in 1930 to Russian parents. He grew up in a community of Russians and other foreigners in Shanghai, China).

8   Most of the *Kharbintsy* (i.e., Russian residents of Kharbin in China) did not meet each other until they came across the border into China during the 1920s and 1930s. Many of them came originally from the vicinity of Moscow and Kiev as a result of the persecution under Tsar Nicholas I. They settled in the areas of *Primorsk* (Maritime District in the Russian Far East), Sakhalin Island, and even northern Japan. Most of the *Sinkiangtsy* (Russian Old Believers of the Sinkiang region in China) came from the Russian-Polish border area, and migrated to the Siberian regions because of persecution in the mid-1700s. They settled in the areas of Kamchatka Peninsula in the Russian Far East, and in Kazakhstan and Uzbekistan in Central Asia.

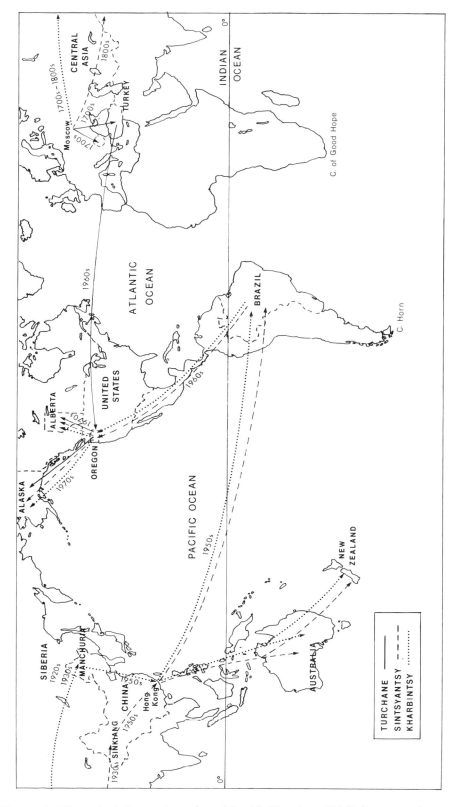

Figure 1. *Historical dispersion of world-wide Russian Old Believer settlements.*

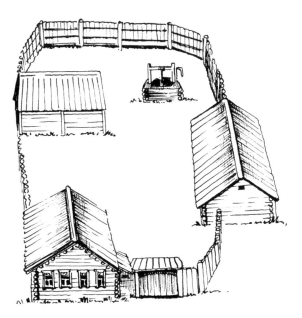

Figure 2. *Traditional Russian Old Believer household.*

Figure 3. *Anisim Kalugin and his wife Solomeya. Nikolaevsk, Alaska, May 1986.*
Photo by Alexander Dolitsky

or single individuals, either escaped or received permission to leave for
Hong Kong, then a territory under jurisdiction of the United Kingdom. The
British, the Red Cross, and the United World Council of Churches provided
assistance in Hong Kong while arrangements were being made for emigration
to other regions of the world. Later, in 1958–59, they relocated from Hong
Kong to various immigrant-seeking countries under sponsorship of the
Intergovernmental Committee for European Migration. In Hong Kong, they
were given the choice of countries they could go to, including Australia, New
Zealand, Brazil, Argentina, Paraguay, Bolivia and Uruguay; the largest groups
went to Brazil and Australia (Figure 1).

The majority of Old Believers arrived in Brazil between 1959–61. There, the
United World Council of Churches provided 6,000 acres of land at Curitiba
(about 200 miles southwest of Sao Paulo) and promised to provide them with
the means and assistance necessary to get started in farming their land (Rearden
1975). Life in Brazil appears to have been difficult from the start. The soil and
climatic conditions were vastly different from anything Old Believers had
known in Russia and China. After several discouraging years of attempting
to adapt to a new bio-physical and socio-cultural environment, some were
able to voluntarily leave for the United States and Canada, with the help of
the Tolstoy Foundation in New York and the personal intervention of U.S.
Attorney General Robert F. Kennedy. Most Old Believers began their migration
to North America in the mid-1960s, between 1964–69. Eventually, most of them
settled in Oregon, where an existing community of Old Believers continues to
prosper. The population has since increased to approximately 10,000 within a
two-county area.

Figure 4. *Entrance to the village of Nikolaevsk, Kenai Peninsula, Alaska, July 1983. Photo by Alexander Dolitsky.*

Today there are eleven *sobors* (prayer halls) in Oregon, reflecting the community's internal social division into three principal sub-groups that migrated from their former residences — *Kharbintsy* from Manchuria and *Sinkiangtsy* from Sinkiang in China, and *Turchany* from Turkey.[9] Within these divisions, they are further subdivided on the basis of kinship groups. Although the Oregon contingent is no longer located in a cohesive village, the Old Believers continue to congregate in prayer halls (*molelnyy dom*) for worship and gather at kin homesteads for marriages and other major socio-cultural events. To attend any of these activities is to re-live aspects of the historical accounts of pre-revolutionary (October 1917) peasant Russia (Morris 1981, 1982).

The most orthodox group, recoiling under the threat of cultural erosion resulting from the compromises necessary to co-exist with the host culture, exercised the ultimate strategy of exodus to a more remote and isolated region. Eventually, in 1967, five Old Believer families (10 adults and 12 children) from Woodburn, Oregon, purchased 640 acres of land and leased an additional two and one-quarter acres of adjacent land on the Kenai Peninsula, along the Anchor River, in Alaska, and began building a community near Anchor Point in the summer of 1968 when the vanguard of families arrived from Oregon. They named this community Nikolaevsk. Two smaller satellite villages in the vicinity were named *Nakhodka* and *Klyuchevaya*. In 1969, the community installed a water system in Nikolaevsk, and connected electricity from the Homer Electric

---

9   The Turkish group left Russia about 230–240 years ago and lived in Turkey until 1963. In 1963, some of them immigrated to the United States. The three groups settled in the same area of Woodburn, Oregon in the 1960s. Although there are minor differences in dialects and customs, they share common cultural traditions, customs, and beliefs.

Association. The group constructed a sawmill to produce the lumber needed to construct houses, barns, sheds and boats for drift fishing (Fortier 1970:34–35). In 1971, 15 of the Old Believers formed the Russian Maritime Company, built a shop in Nikolaevsk, and by 1975 had produced 16 34-foot fiberglass, diesel-powered commercial fishing boats; at least 35 of the villagers became successful commercial fisherman (Rearden 1975:7–9).

Figure 5. *Kondratiy Fefelov, the priest of* popovtsy *grouping in Nikolaevsk, May 1986. Photo by Alexander Dolitsky.*

Figure 6. *Prayer hall* (molelnyy dom) *of the* bespopovtsy *grouping. Nikolaevsk, July 1983 (burned in 1984). Photo by Alexander Dolitsky.*

Figure 7. *Saint Nicholas Church of the* popovtsy *grouping. Nikolaevsk, May 1986. Photo by Alexander Dolitsky.*

In the early 1970s, other families from Oregon split off to form new settlements in northern Canada, near Edmonton, Alberta, and on the Kenai Peninsula and Kodiak Island in the state of Alaska (Figure 1). The Alaskan communities have prospered and grown in the last 50 years from 70 residents in 1970 to a few hundred residents in 1975 and today's population numbers about 2,000 statewide. The Alaska settlements attract families from Oregon and other locations world-wide. Initially founded in 1968 by five families, the village Nikolaevsk has become the largest Old Believer settlement in Alaska (Figure 4). As of June 2015, the village had a population of nearly 400, or about 70–80 nuclear families. The village has a public school that is managed by the state of Alaska and that is attended almost exclusively by Russian-speaking children from Nikolaevsk. The advantage of a cohesive community eased the strain of continual enforcement of traditional cultural norms, values, and behavior.

In the summer of 1983, when I visited Nikolaevsk for the first time, I noticed an emerging controversy in the village between two factions of its residents — priestly and priestless. Two years later, the *Anchorage Daily News* (January 27, 1985: A1, A9–10) reported about the confrontation among Old Believers on the Kenai Peninsula. The conflict centered on differences in religious conduct: some Old Believers, led by Kondratiy Fefelov, who had studied in a monastery in Romania, "uncorrupted," as he stated, "by religious reforms," favored ordaining priests (Figure 5). Many of the villagers, however, refused to accept Fefelov as a priest and denounced his idea. During 1983–84, as a result of this dilemma, five priestless (*bespopovtsy*) nuclear families left Nikolaevsk to establish a new Old Believer settlement, *Berezovka* (birch tree in Russian), in a rural area of interior Alaska near the existing community of Willow.

A while later, on July 6, 1984, the prayer hall (*molelnyy dom*) of the *bespopovtsy* in Nikolaevsk burned to the ground under suspicious circumstances (Figure 6). Kondratiy Fefelov and his nephew Paul were accused by several villagers in this action, but Anchor Point Fire Chief Bob Craig reported that no conclusions were reached on this matter. A few days before the old church (praying house) burned down, a priestly grouping (*popovtsy*), led by priest Kondratiy Fefelov, completed construction of a new church, The Church of Saint Nikolas, according to the theological principles of the *Belokrinitsky Hierarchy* tradition. The new priestly church was built across the street from the original priestless prayer hall that burned down (Figure 7).

The "schism" (*raskol*) of the 1980s in Nikolaevsk has been settled. In protest, the most traditional Old Believers left the estranged community and moved to other remote regions of Alaska. As Andron Martushev (priestless) once told me during my visit to *Berezovka* village in May of 1986, "I want it to be the way it was before the split in the community, I don't want to live near evil." Today, although priestly and priestless groupings' interactions are limited to occasional acknowledgements on the streets of Nikolaevsk and Kachemak Bay, people have learned how to coexist as neighbors and live in peace.

CULTURAL TRADITIONS OF THE 20th-CENTURY RUSSIAN ORTHODOX OLD BELIEVERS

Religious Practices and Restrictions

From the religious point of view, Old Believers represent the pre-17th-century reform Russian Orthodox. They are broadly divided into the *popovtsy* (priestly) or those who recognize priests and have retained the priesthood, and the *bespopovtsy* (priestless), who have no priests. They also are divided into numerous concords, sects, persuasions, ethnic enclaves, and tendencies. In the 18th century, the number of Old Believer sects known to authorities reached around 200 (Stepniak 1977:266 [1888]). Presently, lack of field research and available information precludes documenting all of these factions in any meaningful and complete list. Nevertheless, according to a prominent Russian historian of the 19th century, Sergey Stepniak (1977:275-76 [1888]), the priestless Old Believers in the 19th century could be grouped into four distinct persuasions or branches: (1) The *Pomortsy*, or the sea-shore sects of the northern sea-coast is the oldest and most moderate branch of the priestless which originated in the 17th century in North Russia (East Karelia and Arkhangelsk District); (2) The *Fedoseyevtsy*, separated from the main body of the *Pomortsy* in the beginning of the 18th century, formed another concord of the priestless; (3) The *Beguny* or Wonderers, is the youngest branch of the priestless, and by far more conservative than the first two; (4) The *Filippovtsy* — named after their founder, the monk Filipp — originated in the middle of the 18th century. They share much in common with *Fedoseyevtsy*, but are somewhat more conservative.

In modern Alaska, Oregon, and Trans-Baykal, there are no priests left in the *bespopovtsy* and *Temnovertsy* (Dark-believers) concords. Instead, a *nastoyatel* (layman), who is elected as a spiritual leader, *nastavnik* (mentor), or *nachyotchik* (a person well-read in Scriptures) leads the community. The *nastoyatel* substitutes for a priest by conducting church services, baptisms, and marriage rites, and by teaching *Church Slavonic* grammar and reading to village youth. He is also consulted about spiritual questions and holds confessions. *Semeyskiye-popovtsy* of Trans-Baykal, *popovtsy* in Oregon and Alaska, and the *Austrian* faction of the *popovtsy*, however, do recognize the authority of priests (Heretz 2008). Old Believers, especially *bespopovtsy* concords, strictly adhere to rituals and church writings of the pre-17th-century reform of the Russian Orthodox Church.

Prior to the mid-17th century, religious conduct was developed and taught to the Russians by ascetic Greek monks who emphasized austere deprivation, prolonged worship services resembling all-night vigils, and long, strict fasting periods. Such is the case with Old Believers today. They are left, essentially, with monastic rites. Old Believers greatly cherish their religious rituals and are completely subordinate to their *nastoyatel*, *nastavnik*, or *starets* (elder), who can read *Church Slavonic* and knows Holy Scripture.

Figure 8. *Miriam Lancaster enjoys a conversation with Marina Kalugin. Nikolaevsk, Alaska, August 1989. Photo by Alexander Dolitsky.*

Generally, 44 religious holidays may be celebrated; thus, Old Believers spend many days out of the year in church for at least a few hours each day (*see* Appendix: p. 71 *infra*). Service begins at 2:00 a.m. on Sundays and frequent holidays, and it lasts 6-8 hours; the people attending, except those who are very old, stand through most of the service. The Easter service can last up to 15 hours. The week after Easter is celebrated by all men and women by going from house to house singing in praise of Christ, *Slavit Khrista*, and enjoying the abundant delicacies of homemade food and *braga* (homemade wine) from which they have abstained during the Long Great Fast. The fasting requirements are very long and quite severe. With Wednesdays and Fridays as fasting days, and 44 religious holidays on the church calendar, in addition to four prolonged fasting periods during the year, Old Believers abstain from all animal products, including milk, eggs, lard, butter, cheese, together with wine and oil, a total of over 200 days a year (*see* Appendix: p. 71 *infra*).

Discipline within the family is strict and under the consensual influence of the *sobor*, a church group elected of adult men of the congregation. The *sobor* also elects other church officials and follows traditional rules in making decisions on both spiritual and secular matters. The *sobor* has political power. It approves or denies all suggestions and issues that are brought by residents and that affect the whole community. There is a political hierarchy among Old Believers that constitutes the political aspect of the semi-autonomy of their local communities. On the one hand is the local community, hostile to the outside, sharing certain common rights in land and governed by local, often informal, mechanisms of social control; and, on the other hand, is the hierarchy of patrimonial relations of personal superiority and responsibility, and subordinate dependence, that links the local community with the wider polity.

Obedience to the *startsy* (elders) is a virtue, and the ancient standards and norms define and measure it. When interacting with outsiders, Old Believers are careful not to violate the rules of sacred cleanliness. Most of the time, they do not allow outsiders or those not in the "union" to eat at the same table with them in their homes. Similarly, the most conservative members do not accept food from outsiders. The non-believer guest is treated very hospitably, but is fed separately and served in dishes kept separate and washed separately — often under an outside faucet.

During my many visits to Old Believer households, whether priestly or priestless, my assistants and I were served meals and drinks with disposable paper plates and plastic utensils. On one occasion, when we were called to the supper table, one of the young women said to my assistant Miriam Lancaster:

> *I hope this doesn't offend you but we will be serving your meal on separate plates. They are perfectly fine plates. There is nothing wrong with them. We just believe that because we are baptized we are cleaner than you. I hope this doesn't make you feel bad. Some people don't understand and are offended. It's hard for me to say this.*

Miriam assured the young woman that she "...understands and not to worry, she had not been offended" (Figure 8).

Although there are strict religious prohibitions against the consumption of alcoholic beverages, Old Believers prepare their own home-made wine or *braga* — an alcoholic drink made from raisins, yeast, sugar, and berries. Most Old Believers eschew alcoholic beverages available in the market, but are very generous with their own *braga*. In the home, every meal and often the preparation of various foods and other household tasks must be blessed (Rearden 1972, Morris 1981, 1982).

Church-related ceremonies mark various important parts of an individual's life cycle. At birth, for example, the primary event is the christening. The baby is expected to be delivered by an individual who is among the faithful, which makes many Old Believers apprehensive of delivering their babies in hospitals. There are midwives among Old Believers who usually perform this service for the expectant mother. If these rules are violated, it is believed that an unchristened baby will not see the face of God. The baby is usually christened within eight days after its birth. The ceremony is performed on a holiday or Sunday, whichever occurs within the 8-day limit. A name is chosen for the baby from a list of Saints' days; the parents choose the most suitable name from within the 8-day period. The day of the Saint for whom the child is named becomes the name day of the child.

Many Old Believers (e.g., the *Pomortsy* and *Fedoseyevtsy* groupings in the Baltic States) communicate with the Old Orthodox Church of *Pomorye*, the maritime region in the Baltic Sea (Zhilko and Meks 1997). Russian Orthodox Old Believers in Alaska, however, have no dealings with other branches of the Orthodox Church and do not proselytize. They are unconcerned about whom the world sees as "Real Orthodox." They are solely concerned with their own salvation and believe that God regards them as the "True Orthodox," true believers. There is no hostility on their part toward other Orthodox Christians, or other world religions.

Presently, in modern Alaska—although traditional religious rules strictly forbid Old Believers to smoke, drink hard liquor, use drugs and birth control, to have a childbirth in a public hospital, or for women to use makeup—they are not always in compliance with these religious restrictions.

During interviews in 1989, interviewees explained that, "…there is a lady in the village who helps the women to deliver babies, but she's not a nurse or midwife. She's good about knowing if there is any trouble and sends us to the doctor when necessary. In the village, many babies are born at home. It's so expensive to go to the hospital." She was asked, "Does the church believe in birth control?" She answered, "No, not at all, but many women in our village use birth control. And I don't care, I'm going to use it, too!" The young woman, who was most vocal during this interview, already had three children. "I almost died during my last pregnancy," she said, "and I still have not regained my health." [10]

Marriage, Marital Residence, Kinship, and Divorce

Marriage among Alaskan and Siberian Old Believers does not have a unified procedure or typical pattern. As a rule, Old Believers, even those in Russia, do not practice *venchaniye* (i.e., wedding ceremonies under the Russian Orthodox Church traditions), nor do they acknowledge the legitimacy of civil marriage requirements of the state (Pokrovsky 1974). The *semeyskiye* of Trans-Baykal, for example, are divided into many different sects and some of them refuse to recognize Orthodox Church ceremonies. The *semeyskiye* of the *Austrian* faction of the *popovtsy* and *Beglopopovtsy*, however, confirm their marriages by following Russian Orthodox Church ceremonies, in which the brides are crowned (Popova 1928). The *semeyskiye-popovtsy*, who recognize the authority of the priests of the Orthodox Church, sometimes intermarried with Russian political exiles sent permanently to Siberia by the tsarist government, or with members of the aboriginal population (Blomkvist and Grinkova 1930,

---

10 My assistant, Miriam Lancaster, herself a registered nurse with a public health focus, talked to several women on the subjects of pregnancy, childbirth, and birth control during the August 1989 visit to an Old Believer village. Names of the village and interviewees have been removed to protect their privacy. The visit was in 1989, but the exact date and location of the visit has not been disclosed.

Bolonev 1974). Old Believers from Bukhtarmin Fortress in the Altay Mountains (*Kamenshchiki*) have had prayer halls (*molelnyy dom*), but they confirmed their marriages in the Orthodox Church of the Bukhtarmin Fortress (Mamsik 1975). Only *bespopovtsy* and *Temnovertsy* (Dark-believers) concords ignore priests, and they confirm marriages not under the church, but in the prayer halls within a secret society (Figure 6).

Prior to a marriage, *startsy* (elders) check and calculate the blood relationship of the youth or marriageable prospects. Numerous rules that prohibit marriage are written in the old books. These regulations are predominantly related to kinship relationships, requiring a four-generation gap (*po vosmomu kolenu*) between bride and groom, and subsequently reducing the eligible pool even more than the common pan-cultural restrictions, that say a spouse must be approximately the same age (or the man older), the same *tolk* (religious affiliation), and that both partners have never been married before. Marriage is forbidden if the elder discovers discrepancies or flaws in blood relationships between two prospects (Figure 9).

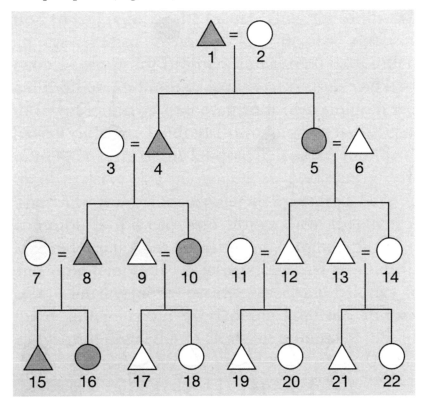

Figure 9. *Four generations of the Old Believer patrilineal descent.*

In this diagram, individuals 1, 4, 5, 8, 10, 15, and 16, represented by the color purple, are affiliated by patrilineal descent; all of the other individuals belong to other patrilineal groups. Individuals 15 through 22 belong to the fourth generation and they are allowed to marry with an opposite sex of the same descent. 15–18 are allowed to marry 19–22 of an opposite sex.

Old Believers in Alaska are of the patrilineal descent and recognize patrilocal residence. Patrilineal descent affiliates an individual with kin of both sexes related to him or her through men only. In patrilineal systems, as with the Old Believers in Alaska, the children in each generation belong to the kin group of their father; the father, in turn, belongs to the group of his father, and so on. Although a man's sons and daughters are all members of the same descent group, affiliation with that group is transmitted only by the sons to their children. Therefore, daughters must leave home when they marry. As Kondratiy Fefelov of Nikolaevsk said, "The son stays and the daughter leaves, so that the married couple lives with or near the husbands's parents. The parents refuse the warm nest to their daughter (*roditeli otkazyvayut tyoploye gnyozdyshko ikh docheri*)."

Figure 10. *Alexander Dolitsky (center) talks with Kondratiy Fefelov (right), the priest of* popovtsy, *and his wife Irina (left) about the structure of Old Believer kinship and kinship terminology. Nikolaevsk, April 2001.*

"The Orthodox Church permits divorce and remarriage. Certainly, Orthodoxy regards the marriage bond as in principle lifelong and indissoluble, and it condemns the breakdown of marriage as a sin and an evil. But while condemning the sin, the Church still desires to help the sinners and to allow them a second chance" (Ware 1986:301).

Old Believers condemn and discourage divorces, but on very rare occasions, when married couples face irreconcilable differences, such as frequent domestic conflicts or chronic and large consumption of alcohol, mostly by male members of the household, the priest of the *popovtsy* or *nastoyatel* (layman) of the *bespopovtsy* will grant a divorce. Nevertheless, as the priest of *popovtsy*, Kondratiy Fefelov, emphasized during one of our meetings in April of 2001, "...there must be a good reason for a couple to petition for a divorce before the church. The church will not grant a divorce only because couples fall out of love with each other; this is not a good reason for breakdown of a family."

Wedding Customs and Ceremonies

Weddings are traditional peasant village affairs. Prior to the actual wedding, typical Russian peasant ceremonies such as the engagement negotiations are carried out by the parents of the bride (*nevesta*) and groom (*zhenikh*). The final agreement is toasted with presents and a drink. Other ceremonies include *devichniki*, the time of increased sewing by the bride and her girlfriends, and the evening parties during which the groom and his friends come to call.

There is also the light-hearted "buying of the bride," in which the groom comes to take her to her new family, and the touching farewell (*proshchaniye*) of the bride to her parents. The wedding party, with a "chain" of handkerchiefs, proceeds to the prayer hall of *bespopovtsy* or to the church of *popovtsy*. The *venchaniye*, or crowning ceremony, takes place after the regular Sunday service, and the wedding (*svadba*) is celebrated for three consecutive days at the home of the groom's father. The bride's dowry trunk (*sunduk*) is delivered by her kinsmen and "sold" to the wedding party.

Later, after a meal (*pir* or *obed*), the young couple stands for the bowing ceremony (*poklony*), which is the opportunity for kin to give them wise advice and numerous presents. On the last day of the wedding, the young couple must "buy" the presents from the best man (*svidetel*) and the matrons of honor with kisses, bows and witticisms. At this point, the bride's mother-in-law (*tyoshcha*) is also auctioned off (Morris 1981, 1982).

"After the regular service has ended, everyone leaves except for the bride, groom, the members of their "chain," the parents of the bride and groom, the *nastoyatyel*, and three or four other male witnesses. None of the younger and unmarried people are supposed to see the wedding ceremony itself, and the first wedding an Old Believer sees is usually their own. The bride and groom are asked once again three times if they are marrying of their free will, and if they answer "yes," then the ceremony begins in earnest. After an initial prayer said in unison, the bride and groom exchange rings, naming each other husband and wife. They are then blessed by their parents, who present them with the icons which have been chosen from among the supplies of both families, to be given to the newlyweds for their own household. While the blessings are being administered, the couple kneels before the parents of both families.

"After this, the bride is taken to the back of the church where her marriage-cap (*shashmura*) and scarves are laid out on a dresser. She removes her *krassota* (the crown), which she has been wearing all through the ceremony, and the bridesmaids then plait her hair into two braids, tie them up over her head, and place the *shashmura* over it and two scarves over that. The bride is now given the appearance of a married woman, since unmarried women and girls wear their hair in a single braid down the back. She is never to show her hair to any man other than her husband, according to traditional decree.

"She then proceeds to the groom, and bows before him to the floor, and kisses him. This is to indicate, symbolically, that she is now his and that she will be loyal and submissive toward him for the rest of her days. The "chain" then forms again, while the *nastoyatyel* reads the portions of the sacred texts which describe the duties of wife and husband toward each other and toward their future children. The bride then says a prayer and asks her parents their forgiveness for leaving them to become a member, in essence, of the groom's family. After a closing group prayer, the ceremony is finished and the people go to the groom's house for breakfast" (Wigowsky 1978).[11]

Because weddings are meant to be elaborate, plentiful and lavish, they cannot be held on any of the fast days or during the Lenten periods. This tends to make the wedding a seasonal event, normally scheduled just before the 7-week Easter Lent. The groom's family prepares a variety of foods and makes sure that they have plenty of home-made alcoholic drink — *braga*.

Household and Subsistence Activities

The household of Old Believers in many ways is similar to those of the 18th- and 19th-century Siberian peasants of Russian origin. The Trans-Baykalians build their houses with constructive and decorative elements characteristic of the northern areas of Russia and decorate the interior with red, blue, green, and orange colors, using patterns well-known in Ukraine and Belorussia. The Trans-Baykal area is the only place where architectural elements mentioned in folk descriptions of the homesteads of *boyars* (grand dukes or Old-Russian noblemen) still survive (Kuzmina 1982, 1983).

Old Believers in Alaska are not exceptionally tradition-bound in their household construction. Generally, the Old Believers of Nikolaevsk live in large, one-story houses consisting of several rooms, a kitchen, small closets and a veranda (Figure 11). Several small buildings such as *banya* (steam baths), *stoybishche* (cattle house), *parnik* (heated green house) and toilet are within the area of a nuclear family's household. Each family household constitutes an independent economic unit and is surrounded by a solidly built fence. Furniture in the main house is quite simple, but strong and comfortable. Although some elements of the traditional architecture and interior design are still present

---

11 Paul J. Wigowsky, a Russian-speaking school teacher with many years of experience in teaching Old Believer students in Hubbard, Oregon, has written an extensive, well-researched, and reliable description of Old Believer faith, history, and traditional lifestyles (Wigowsky 1978).

within Old Believer households, modern utilities are favored and extensively used by Old Believers of all religious groupings (Figure 12). An altar with the family icons sitting in a small shelter, curtained with an embroidered covering, stands in a prominent corner of the front room.

Alaskan Old Believers' economic success can be explained by values that confer normative status on hard work, modest needs, and efficient management of household resources. Old Believers value property and wealth, not as necessities in themselves, but as insurance against possible future hardship. If necessary, Old Believers often assist each other, especially within related nuclear families. Clusters of closely related families are the cornerstones of the community.

The religious and social isolation of Old Believers in Alaska is a major determinant of their quasi-subsistence living conditions. Presently, in contrast to the Amish, Old Believers are not in competition with new technology – i.e., machinery, appliances, electricity, telephones, and other advances. However, Old Believers are economically, mostly agriculturally, self-sufficient. Yet, they are efficient as well. Many conservative families do not purchase food (except sugar, salt and flour) or traditional clothes outside of their community. Each family tries to guarantee its supply of food for the entire year. Their food comes largely from vegetable gardening, fishing, cattle raising, and hunting. The basic diet is made up of home-grown vegetables, bread and pastries made from wheat and corn, meat that is approved if it comes from an animal with a cloven hoof, fish and shellfish.[12] None of the Alaskan Old Believers make their living from farming, primarily because of cold and long winters and the short growing season in Alaska.

Trade and exchange play a vital role in Old Believers' daily life, penetrating the social system and holding the community together. Sometimes Old Believers buy or trade a particular essential item within their community. For example, in the 1980s, Andron Martushev's family, residents of the Alaskan village of Nikolaevsk, supplied milk to their relatives, Fedor Basargin's family. Similarly, Fedor's family sold skillfully tailored traditional garments, made by his wife, Irina, to Andron and other villagers. Balanced reciprocity is a common form of direct exchange among Old Believers in which goods and services flow two ways. One party gives a gift to another party with an expectation of the return of a gift of equivalent value within a particular period of time. These relationships decrease and eventually disappear among people who are geographically and kinship-wise remote from each other.

Some families specialize in certain subsistence activities such as fishing, carpentry, or shipbuilding (Figure 13). The subsistence specialization reflects the household and structure of the farms. Often nuclear families from the same religious sect cooperate to negotiate a large construction contract from

---

12 Among conservative Old Believers in Alaska, animals with paws (e.g., squirrel, rabbit, and bear) are regarded as unfit to eat.

Figure 11. *Old Believer Household. Nikolaevsk, April 2001. Photo by Alexander Dolitsky.*

Figure 12. *Solomeya Kalugin uses modern kitchen appliances. Nikolaevsk, August 1989. Photo by Alexander Dolitsky.*

Figure 13. *Shipbuilding, Inc., Nikolaevsk, May 1986. Photo by Alexander Dolitsky.*

outside the village. The main economic factor of such cooperation, as a rule, is a religious solidarity among relevant Old Believer sects and factions. Normally, Old Believers do not carry out business and trade with opposing Orthodox sects.

Appearance

As is the case with nearly every other aspect of Old Believers' lives, the traditions of appearance have religious significance and, historically, are deeply rooted in the medieval past. The physical type and outer appearance of Old Believers is Slavic. The Old Believers of Trans-Baykal, as well as most conservative North American Old Believers, wear clothing reminiscent of the 17th and 18th centuries, despite the stylistic differences of their clothes, reflecting different cultural and geographical origins (Figures 14, 15, 16). Turkish and southern European traditions influenced some styles of Old Believers' clothing, especially women's daily dress. At baptism, however, a person is dressed in a shirt bound with a belt and is given a cross to wear around the neck. These three traditional elements — the shirt (*rubashka*), belt (*poyas*), and cross (*krest*) — must be worn at all times in public (Uspensky 1905, Eliasov 1963, Morris 1981, 1982). The main apparel items of religious significance are the *poyas* (woven belt) and the cross around the neck. These two items symbolize the bond between the bearer and Christ. The belt is not taken off except for bathing or sleeping, and the cross is not taken off except in the event of the replacement of a chain (Figures 14, 15, 16). Men are seen with the long Russian *rubashka*, a tunic-like shirt girded with a

Figure 14. *Ulita Kalugin (left) is wearing a* sarafan *and her mother Solomeya (right) is wearing a* talichka, *Alexander Dolitsky (center). Nilkolaevsk, May 1986. Photo by Alexander Dolitsky.*

Figure 15. *Fedor Basargin, his daughter Ulita, and wife Irina. Nikolaevsk, July 1983. Photo by Alexander Dolitsky.*

Figure 16. *Trans-Baykal Old Believers in the early-20ᵗʰ century. Collection of Alexander Dolitsky.*

poyas, a woven belt. The women wear a full dress over a long-sleeved blouse and full-length slips. Women lengthen the blouse to form a blouse/slip combination and wear a jumper *(sarafan)*[13] over it, or *talichka*[14] along with the ever-present peasant apron, as illustrated in Figures 14, 15 and 16 (Grinkova 1930, Eliasov 1963, Morris 1982). Children wear the adult-style clothing in smaller sizes (Figures 17, 18). Holiday clothing is more fanciful and colorful, but in the same style (Matros 1827, Rozen 1870, Grinkova 1930, Morris 1981, 1982).

Men cut their hair, except for a fringe in front, and leave their beards untrimmed. In their religious books, they are enjoined neither to cut their hair at the temples nor to trim the edges of their beards, for to do so would be to deface the likeness of God, in whose image they were created. Old Believers believe that "…a beard is inevitably implied by the notion of man as a reflection of God" (Carmichael 1968:80). Women, according to religious rules, are never permitted to cut their hair. They are not allowed to show their arms above the wrists, their legs above the calf, or any other part of their bodies in public. Unmarried women plait their hair in a single braid, and, after marriage, they keep it bound with two braids under a cap *(shashmura)* covered with a kerchief. The purpose of the *shashmura* is to hold the hair in place; women's hair is long — sometimes past their knees. When they wash it, they braid it into two braids and wrap it around their head while it is still wet. Hence, in the town, on the streets and in residential areas, one is treated to the frequent sight of Russians, resembling peasants of yesteryear, nonchalantly going about their business.

For Old Believers, appearance becomes highly symbolic of one's attachment to the group and one's place within society. Traditional dress becomes identified and integrated with a total way of life, and the manner of dressing becomes one of the most important elements of their collective consciousness and representation.

Language

Old Believer language and stories reflect their life in the North, the picturesque landscapes, and their socio-economic contacts with non-Russian nationalities.

---

13 The *sarafan* is the traditional dress of the Russian Old Believers in Alaska (*see* Figure 14, left). It is an all-purpose piece of clothing, serving both as the everyday work dress and as the dress for formal occasions. The *sarafan* consists of a long skirt and a bodice with shoulder straps. It is worn with a blouse, which provides the sleeves and collar. A belt is always worn around the waist. Often an apron is worn with the *sarafan*, especially on more formal occasions. Unlike the *talichka* (*see* Figure 14, right), the design of the *sarafan* has not lent itself to many modern revisions.

14 The *talichka* is a non-traditional Russian dress, a variation of the *sarafan* adapted in China (*see* Figure 14, right and Figure 15). The *talichka* is never worn in church or prayer hall, and in some conservative communities the policy is not to allow the *talichka* on any occasion, even for casual wear. Through her choice of wearing a *sarafan* or *talichka*, an Old Believer woman makes a statement about her views on the traditional social values of the community she represents.

Figure 17. *Children wear the adult style clothing sized for them, Basargin's family. Nikolaevsk, July 1983. Photo by Alexander Dolitsky.*

Figure 18. *Children wear the adult style clothing sized for them, Kalugin's family. Nikolaevsk, May 1986. Photo by Alexander Dolitsky.*

Figure 19. *Pilogeya Fefelov and her two sons, Semyon (4 years old) and Danikt (3 years old), in the kitchen of Kondratiy Fefelov's home, August, 1989. Photo by Alexander Dolitsky.*

It should be noted, however, that some elements of the Siberian way of life and vocabulary persist only in the descriptions of material culture. Poetry, reflecting the spiritual life of the epic heroes, remains unchanged and is preserved as a precious relic, even when words and expressions have lost their relation to former life situations and have become outdated.

North American Old Believers speak Russian at home and in most work places. Although only a few Alaskan Old Believers were born in Russia or in Russian-speaking communities abroad (i.e., China, Japan, South America), the Russian language is very much alive. Given the size of Russian communities in Oregon and Alaska, there is ample opportunity for Russian speakers to form groups for contract work outside of their villages, reducing the need to learn English as a second language. Living in neighborhood clusters in rural Alaska, there is little need for members, especially women who remain at home and have little interaction with the outside world, to speak English. Parents encourage their children to speak Russian at home and to have minimal interaction with English-speaking outsiders, so there is limited opportunity to practice English at home.

During an interview, my assistant, Miriam Lancaster, observed and recorded two children learning Russian and English at home (Figures 19 and 20):

Figure 20. *Semyon and Danikt Fefelovs are enjoying our visit, August, 1989. Photo by Alexander Dolitsky.*

As we were putting the puzzles together and coloring, I asked two children the colors of various things. The older child would always respond in perfect English. When I asked the younger child, he just smiled and the older would whisper the word in English into the younger child's ear. The younger would smile bigger and say the color in English. I told the children's mother that I was surprised that the older child could speak English so well since he wasn't old enough to be in school. The mother said she only speaks Russian to him at home because she's afraid he will forget their language. She said the only place he hears English is on TV from "Sesame Street" and "Mr. Rogers." It also surprised me that the child knew to speak only English to me. The older child and I spoke quite a lot and he never mixed a Russian word with English. When speaking to everyone else in the room, he spoke Russian.

Today, anyone over the age of 60 who has not attended public school and has had limited exposure to English-speaking people, predominantly speaks Russian. Their conversational Russian is quite fluent, with a relatively extensive vocabulary, similar to the language of Siberian peasants with South-European Russian dialect. Since the language of groups from Turkey and Romania includes many Ukrainian, Turkish and Polish words as well as East European dialectic variations, mixed with a common English vocabulary, it is sometimes difficult for researchers trained in contemporary Russian language to understand or identify the Old Believer dialect.

Church Slavonic is used for religious services and the young learn to read and chant from their parents and older siblings. It is considered prestigious for Old Believers to read books in *Church Slavonic* during worship and religious holidays and parents always admire such an effort.

Despite heavy Americanization in North America, the Russian language, as a symbol representing an idea, national identity or quality of life, is the channel by which Old Believers communicate beliefs and attitudes to children, clarifying the place they are to take as adults in the community and the world.

Education and Schooling

While the law of the dominant culture, whether in the United States, the former Soviet Union or in Russia, has always required the young to attend public schools, parents have been somewhat apathetic about sending their children to public schools. In fact, many Old Believers still have an uneasy feeling of inferiority in matters of ecclesiastic learning. There are frequent religious holidays when children, as well as their parents, attend church in the early morning hours, conflicting with the school schedule. The school schedule in Nikolaevsk village, Alaska, however, is adjusted according to religious demands and practices of the community, since most students are Old Believers.

Twelve greatly significant Old Believer Religious Holy Days are included in the school calendar, in addition to the regular school holiday/vacation days. The Old Believers' twelve Holy Days during the school year in Nikolaevsk, Alaska are: 8/19—Transfiguration of Christ; 8/28—Assumption of the Mother of God; 9/11—Beheading of St. John the Baptist; 10/9—St. John the Theologian; 10/14—Protection of Mother of God; 12/4—Presentation of Mother of God; 12/19—St. Nicholas of Wonderworker; 1/7—Birth of Christ; 1/19—*Kreshchensky Sochelnik* (The Eve of Epiphany); 5/13—Mid-Pentecost Wednesday; 5/21—St. John the Theologian; and 5/28—Holy Ascension (The Holy Ascension Great Feast is movable every year).

The total enrollment at the Nikolaevsk state-operated K-12 school is about 140 students, between 110–20 are Russian Old Believers (Figure 21). There are 2-4 Old Believers teachers who teach Russian language and the school board is formed primarily from Old Believers who control school curriculum, requirements and, to some degree, the school's internal environment.

Older children are often kept at home to look after younger siblings, with large nuclear families commonly having 6–12 children. Many Old Believer parents are apprehensive about the exposure their children receive at school. There is outright objection to subjects they consider offensive, including science, sex education, music, contemporary art, literature, and aerobics. They also often complain that the school environment tends to weaken the disciplined behavior required of their children. Parents frequently urge teachers to

Figure 21. *Old Believers play baseball at the school playground, Nikolaevsk, May 1986. Photo by Alexander Dolitsky.*

be stricter with their children, encouraging them to use physical punishment when necessary (Morris 1981, 1982).

Today, a shortage of job opportunities in the villages has resulted in many Old Believers leaving their traditional communities to move to urban areas of Alaska. Here they raise their families in predominately non-Russian speaking neighborhoods. It is common to see young Old Believer families at public recreation facilities, including swimming pools, skating rinks, and parks. Children of Old Believer families living in urban areas attend public schools as minorities, with non-Russian students, in contrast to public schools in Old Believer villages where most students are from Old Believer families. Parents of students attending schools in urban areas provide school administrators with information about traditional practices, religious restrictions, and a schedule of religious holidays that must be observed by their children during the academic year. School administrators accommodate these requests with sincere understanding and respect for Old Believers' culture.

In the last 20–25 years some Old Believers, both male and female, have received a college education or vocational training and many young have left their traditional community. However, Old Believers, generally, retain a characteristic Russian peasant attitude toward public education; namely, that the young should learn to read, write, and think so as not to be cheated by shopkeepers and hostile neighbors. Any more abstract learning is in

God's realm and should be left alone. Consequently, parents have regularly withdrawn their children from public schools after the sixth grade, at a time when the offensive subjects are offered and when children's labor becomes essential to the family budget and livelihood.

Their formal education brought to a halt, children are given simple household responsibilities when very young, and they turn their attention to full-time adult work along with their parents. As a general rule, they achieve adulthood early and are encouraged to marry early as well. For boys, the marriage age is about 17–22, and for girls, the age is usually between 15–20, or sometimes as young as 13. Early marriage and full-time work are thought to have advantages; they keep the young busy with adult responsibilities. The newlyweds frequently become parents within the first year. Thus, they have an obligation to abide by the religious rules to keep themselves in the "union," if for no other reason than to be eligible to baptize their children. It is believed that the young will be protected from the temptations of the host cultures by occupying themselves with church and family, and in remaining self-sufficient. All of this takes time, and both causes and necessitates interaction with "one's own kind," preserving the hierarchy of authority and conservative social orders within the community.

DISCUSSION

Embedded as it is within cultures characterized by increasing structural-functional differentiation, unilinear evolutionary theory would predict that Old Believer society would be evolving in much the same fashion. Specialization of its social structure should become increasingly congruent with the broader institutional environment. As the foregoing ethnographic description demonstrates, however, Old Believer society has only slowly assimilated the increasing complexity that characterizes its larger, enveloping cultural environment in the United States. In this regard, Old Believers share similarity with many other religious refugees and cultural enclaves embedded within modern systems, such as the Amish, Hutterites, *Dukhobors* and Orthodox Jews in North America.

Rather than high levels of structural-functional differentiation and "organic solidarity," minimal levels of structural complexity characterize Old Believer society. The institutions of religion and the family are the paramount determinants of their social behavior. With the exception, perhaps, of education, other institutional patterns, such as occupational participation, legal functions, medical roles, and political decision-making structures, are only minimally disembodied from the ascriptive ties of kinship and religion. Old Believer society is, thus, bound together by the "mechanical solidarity" of collective representations and similar religious values, that characterize less differentiated social structures. As such, Old Believer culture in Alaska remains little changed from its earlier heritage. As a result, Old Believer culture remains highly incongruent with the cultural *milieu* in which it currently resides.

How can the apparent anomaly of Old Believers be accounted for in terms of evolutionary theory? What implications does the existence of Old Believers have for theories of cultural evolution? First, of course, Old Believer culture has evolved somewhat in the past 350 years. Life in close contact to atheistic Soviet ideology, aboriginal populations of China, Brazil, the United States and the former Soviet Union, and the influence of modern technologies and values of the United States and Canada have led to disobedience of traditional ways among Old Believers' youth. Despite a value structure strongly favoring cultural persistence and stability, they have gradually institutionalized practical ideas and elements of modern technologies (e.g., telephones, automobiles, home appliances, and even television among some families) into their social structure. In fact, the rate of change and its impact on religious life have appalled elders and middle-aged parents. Compared to the meager degree of change in cultural life over the past 350 years, changes related to the persistent and unified strategy of the former Soviet government, and the constant exposure to socio-technological changes taking place in the United States were and remain quite rapid and unsettling. Although the oldest generation of Old Believers attempts to isolate its children from the temptations of technologically developed societies by not allowing television, radio, modern music and contemporary literature at home, and by controlling daily life within the community, elements of contemporary Russian and American cultures penetrate into their system and, occasionally, become incorporated into their social structure. These minimal levels of change notwithstanding, how can the persistence of Old Believer culture in the midst of strong social forces toward modernization be explained? To account for this apparent anomaly, we must return to a discussion of evolutionary theory.

Evidently, theories of social evolution borrowed too heavily and uncritically from counterparts in the biological sciences and the historical determinist approach. Whereas the evolutionary sequence of biological systems is characterized by blind variation and selective retention of traits possessing survival value, I ascribe to the view that processes of rational preselection more accurately characterize human systems, in which complex evolutionary problems are anticipated. "They may then beat natural selection to the draw by making their own deliberate adaptive choices, where the advantage of doing so is perceptually obvious. Such decisions occur both at the individual level and through political processes at the group level" (Boehm 1978:265).

Post-Durkheimian theoretical analysis is nearly unanimous in rejecting the reason postulated by Durkheim as the sole cause of the division of labor, namely, competition resulting from physical and moral density as inadequate. Smelser (1959, 1963) argued that the obsolescence of existing structures in the face of new functional requirements is perhaps the major determinate cause of structural-functional differentiation. Most importantly, from the standpoint of this research, however, Eisenstadt's (1970) analysis indicates that one factor serving to stimulate or retard structural-functional differentiation is the activity of powerful elites, such as community elders who control the adoption and/or rejection of new culture traits. Reuschemeyer (1974, 1977) builds on Eisenstadt's conceptualization by broadening it into a more generalized discussion of power. He argues that processes of differentiation (and, significantly, dedifferentiation and persistence) can be understood better by focusing on the role of power constellations and power interests. He argues that processes of dedifferentiation and persistence are strongly influenced by holders of power as they seek to maintain their privilege and status in the face of threatening new values and institutional structures. Power holders, through their ability to influence the introduction of new culture traits or the persistence of existing ones, are thus said to be one of the proximate causes of these processes (Muth 1985).

In a society characterized by similar sentiments and a strong collective conscience, the council of elders and other community leaders are the primary decision-makers for adopting or rejecting new cultural traits, that the culture system comes into contact with, either through invention, accident, or diffusion. This is because these "elites" control the normative cultural prescriptions governing the system. This lends support to the views of Reuschemeyer (1977) and Eisenstadt (1970) concerning the importance of power structures in the process of differentiation, dedifferentiation, and persistence (Muth 1985).[15]

Two adaptive strategies, which appear to have been rationally preselected by Old Believers for their survival value, are: (1) migration and (2) elaborate mechanisms of ethnic boundary maintenance. As Durkheim (1933 [1893]) and others (e.g., Schnore 1958) have noted, migration is one strategy available to members of a system under stress from increasing physical and moral density. The migration patterns of Old Believers appear to support this view. Rather than differentiate their social structure by adding new cultural traits that may conflict with traditional religious and family values, segments of Old Believer settlements periodically split off and migrate elsewhere, thus alleviating the potential conflict resulting from competitive pressures of increasing population, more frequent social contact with unfriendly cultures, and, especially, religious conflict arising within their own system (Scheffel 1989). However, according to Morris' observation:

> In the past, most moves in this group could be accounted for by religious persecution from outsiders. In Turkey, they moved because they couldn't find other Old Believers for marriages. In Woodburn, Oregon, there have been several attempts to find a 'village' area so they could leave the 'mixed' environment where they live. There is a strong preference for community and for a community cohesiveness. The 'priest' split is doctrinal, and has resulted in a re-structuring into renewed cohesive groups. (Richard Morris, personal correspondence, November 28, 1986).

Of equal importance are ethnic boundary maintenance features of Old Believer settlements. Although they are eroding somewhat in Russia and Oregon where Old Believer settlements have existed for a longer period, they are still very much in evidence in the Old Believer settlements in Alaska. These ethnic boundaries set Old Believer settlements apart from proximate communities in the host cultures and serve as filters for cultural traits and institutions introduced from the outside social environment. As Barth (1998:14) has observed regarding ethnic boundary maintenance strategies:

> It is important to recognize that although ethnic categories take cultural differences into account, we can assume no simple one-to-one relationship between ethnic units and cultural similarities and differences. The features that are taken into account are not the sum of 'objective' differences, but only those which the actors themselves regard

---

15 Richard Morris believes that Old Believers in Oregon form a consensual group, where decisions are usually made through unanimous group consent. According to Morris, "…when changes in the community occur, more often than not, it is the women who object. The basic authority is in the patriarchal families, but not in an authoritarian 'elite' of the group" (Richard Morris, personal correspondence, November 28, 1986).

as significant. Not only do ecological variations mark and exaggerate differences; some cultural features are used by the actors as signals and emblems of differences. The cultural contents of ethnic dichotomies would seem analytically to be of two orders: (i) overt signals [or] signs — the diacritical features that people look for and exhibit to show identity, often such features as dress, language, house-form, or general style of life, and (ii) basic value orientations: the standards of morality and excellence by which performance is judged.

As I have attempted to show in the ethnographic descriptions of Old Believer settlements, many of the overt signals preserved by Old Believers are reminiscent of the Russian peasantry of the 17th and 18th centuries. The value system also is reflective of this heritage. To be identified as an Old Believer, individual members maintain and defend these overt signals and values against threats posed by exposure to host cultures. These boundary maintenance strategies further inhibit the intrusion of cultural traits, which might dilute, confuse, or detract from this rather discrete ethnic identity. To again quote Barth (1998:15):

What is more, the ethnic boundary canalizes social life—it entails a frequently quite complex organization of behavior and social relations. The identification of another person as a fellow member of an ethnic group implies a sharing of criteria for evaluation and judgement. It thus entails the assumption that the two are fundamentally 'playing the same game', and this means that there is between them a potential for diversification and expansion of their social relationship to cover eventually all different sectors and domains of activity. On the other hand, a dichotomization of others as strangers, as members of another ethnic group, implies a recognition of limitations on shared understandings, differences in criteria for judgement of value and performance, and a restriction of interaction to sectors of assumed common understanding and mutual interest.

Old Believers in Alaska appear to have negotiated a successful relationship with their dominant host cultures. It remains to be seen how far into the future the strategies by which they have maintained their cultural identity will retain adaptive strength. Forces of change are exerting powerful pressures on Old Believers to modify their traditional ways. I observed that the persistence of Old Believer settlements does not entail a rejection of Durkheimian theories of evolutionary culture change. It does, however, necessitate the adjustment of existing theoretical paradigms to incorporate the concept of rational preselection in order to explain processes of evolutionary development and persistence. In this regard, I agree with Boehm (1978) that rational preselection is inadequately accounted for by ethnologists and that further research and testing are necessary to make the study of processes of culture change and culture continuity conform to empirical reality. Old Believers exercise a rational preselection of culture traits in order to preserve their existing culture. This stands in stark contrast to certain Arctic and Sub-Arctic peoples who embrace the institutions and traits of host cultures. In this regard, Old Believer settlements and experiences may present alternatives to Arctic and Sub-Arctic peoples who are increasingly subsumed by the encroachment of modern societies on their traditional lifestyle.

CONCLUSION

Relying on ethnographic observations and oral testimonies of North American and, partly, Siberian (Trans-Baykal) communities, and the examination of limited written primary and secondary sources, I conclude that Russian Old Believers have experienced social, economic, and ideological upheavals that permit them to embrace or resist new religious modes and cultural modernization. Old Believers have a strong sense of obligation to preserve the age-old religious rituals of the pre-reform Russian Orthodox Church. They have developed a sense of religious identity and attachment in an attempt "… to secure coherence in their universe of relations, both physical and social" (Firth 1951:25).

Lacking more pronounced degrees of cultural differentiation, Old Believers characteristically exhibit a somewhat different pattern of stratification. Old Believers do not seem to feel the same degree of ambivalence toward the political superstructure that other North Americans do. Not having a highly differentiated culture, they do not feel judged by outsiders using a set of standards that they cannot or do not wish to attain. Subsequently, there is less development of a differentiated culture as a kind of 'counter-culture.'

Old Believers have developed ways of dealing with people of superior wealth, power, and prestige, whether these people are officials, wealthy landlords, merchants, or simply educated people who know the world outside of the Old Believer universe and are able to operate effectively in it. Some progressive (i.e., liberal-minded or less conservative) Old Believers seek ties with such people in order to gain increased economic security, to have political protection, and to have an influential person on whom they can rely for guidance in dealing with people and institutions in the wider society.

Old Believers are not quite politically and economically self-sufficient. To some degree, they depend on a wide network of people and institutions with whom they interact and from whom they purchase the goods and services that they themselves do not produce. Old Believers live in a social world in which they are economically and politically disadvantaged. They have neither sufficient capital nor power to make an impression on the urban society. They have no illusions about their position and use all available devices to protect their rights and their socio-economic boundaries.

Certainly, Old Believers in Alaska have changed in some ways over the years. The greatest changes have been in matters of material, technological, and secular culture and social life, and those reflect adaptation to circumstances rather than fundamental alteration of their cultural identity. Religious matters and values have been the most stable elements of their culture. To Old Believers, religion is not an institution parallel to economics, politics, or kinship, but it is the soul of their society; it is more fundamental than other elements, and permeates all of them. For Alaskan Old Believers, religion is not limited to a particular sphere of life; it is all pervasive and dominates everything. Religion determines their values, appearance, eating habits, the roles of children, women and other adults of their society; it shapes their social behavior and subsistence practices.

Their insistence on preservation of the 17th-century pre-reform rituals of the Russian Orthodox Church has resulted in persecution and constant dislocation during the past 350 years. In the United States, particularly in Alaska, they have found religious and traditional freedom, economic survival, a sense of belonging, and state protection of their cultural values. In June 1975, fifty-nine Old Believers of Nikolaevsk village became citizens of the United States. The naturalization ceremony took place at the Anchor Point school near their homes. "After the ceremony, Kiril Martushev spoke for all of the villagers:

> *For a long time, we have looked for a place in the world where we could live our own lives and be free in our beliefs in God. We have found what we were looking for here, and that is why we decided to become citizens of this great United States.*

There was scarcely a dry eye in sight when Kiril sat down" (Rearden 1975:9).

The temptations of the modern and secular world, however, are a constant threat to the discipline and religious loyalty of the youth. In response, some members have moved to more remote locations of the state — *Voznesenka* village in the Kachemak Bay area and *Berezovka* village in south-central Alaska. Old Believers feel that as long as they can stay together as a cohesive community, they will be able to protect their religious freedom and their religious and ethnic identity, to strengthen their economic security, and continue to maintain control over the direction of their lives. Consequently, the Old Believer system of communication with each other and with outsiders, and their strategy of cognitive rational preselection, migration, and boundary maintenance may present lessons and alternatives to other ethnic minorities or isolated communities in Alaska, across the United States and around the world, increasingly being subsumed by the encroachment of urbanization, rapid modernization, global corporate colonization, and Westernization.

BIBLIOGRAPHY

ALBERT, ETHEL M.
  1956   "The Classification of Values: A Method and Illustration, *American Anthropologist*, 58:221–248.

AXTELL, JAMES
  1979   "Ethnohistory: An Historian's Viewpoint," *Ethnohistory*, 26(1):1–13.

BARTH, FREDRIK
  1998   "Introduction." In: *Ethnic Groups and Boundaries: The Social Organization of Culture Difference*, Fredrik Barth, ed. Long Grove, Illinois: Waveland Press, Inc.

BENNETT, JOHN W.
  1969   *Northern Plainsmen: Adaptive Strategy and Agrarian Life*. Chicago: AHM Publishing Co.

  1976   *The Ecological Transition: Cultural Anthropology and Human Adaptation*. New York: Pergamon Press, Inc.

BLOMKVIST, YU. E. and GRINKOVA, N.P.
  1930   "Kto takiye bukhtarminskiye staroobryadtsy?" [Who are the Bukhtarmin Old Believers?]. In: *Bukhtarminskiye Staroobryadtsy* [Bukhtarmin Old Believers], Sergey I. Rudenko, ed. Leningrad: AN SSSR, 17:1–48.

BOAS, FRANZ
  1932   *Anthropology and Modern Life*. (Revised Edition). New York: Macmillan

  1938   *The Mind of Primitive Man*. (Revised Edition). New York: Free Press.

BOEHM, CHRISTOPHER
  1978   "Rational Preselection from Hamadryads to *Homo Sapiens*: The Place of Decisions in Adaptive Process," *American Anthropologist*, 80:266–97.

BOLONEV, F.F.
  1974   *Khozyaistvennye i Bytovye Svyazi Semeyskikh s Mestnym i Prishlym Naseleniyem Buryatii XIX i Nachala XX Vekov* [Socio-economic Contacts Between *Semeyskiye* Old Believers and Local Population of Buryatia in the 19th and Beginning of the 20th Centuries]. In: *Etnographiya*. Ulan Ude: AN SSSR 6:56–68.

BROMLEY, YU. V.
  1979   "Subject Matter and Main Trends of Investigation of Culture by Soviet Ethnographers," *Arctic Anthropology*, 16(1):46-61.

  1983   *Ocherki Teorii Etnosa* [The Theories of Ethnos]. Moscow: Nauka.

BROMLEY, YU. V. and MARKOVA, G.I.
1982   *Etnographiya* [Ethnography]. Moscow: *Vysshaya Shkola* Press.

CARMICHAEL, JOEL
1968   *A Cultural History of Russia.* New York: Weybright and Talley.

CARNEIRO, ROBERT
1962   "Scale Analysis as an Instrument for the Study of Cultural Evolution," *Southwestern Journal of Anthropology*, 18:149–169.

1967   "On the Relationship between Size of Population and Complexity of Social Organization," *Southwestern Journal of Anthropology*, 23:234-243.

and TOBIAS, S.
1963   "The Application of Scale Analysis to the Study of Cultural Evolution" In: *Transactions*, New York Academy of Sciences, Series II, 26:196-207.

CHERNIAVSKY, MICHAEL
1966   "The Old Believers and the New Religion," *Slavic Review,* March issue 25(1):1–40.

COOK, CHRIS
1990   *Dictionary of Historical Terms.* New York: Macmillian Press.

CRUMMEY, ROBERT O.
1970   *The Old Believers and The World of Antichrist: The Vyg Community of the Russian State 1694-1855.* Madison, Milwaukee, and London: The University of Wisconsin Press.

DEREVYANKO, A.B., A.F. FELINGER and YU. P. KHOLYUSHKIN
1989   *Metody Informatiki v Arkheologii Kamennogo Veka* [Methods of Information in the Archaeology of the Stone Age]. Novosibirsk: Nauka.

DOLITSKY, ALEXANDER B.
1984   "Soviet Studies of Northern Peoples," *Current Anthropology*, 25(4):502–503.

1985   "Siberian Paleolithic Archaeology: Approaches and Analytic Methods," *Current Anthropology*, 26(3):361–78.

1990   "*Glasnost* Digs Out from the Past: A Personal View," *SAA*, 8(4):7.

1994   *Change, Stability, and Values in the World of Culture: A Case from Russian Old Believers in Alaska.* 2nd edition. Juneau: Alaska–Siberia Research Center, Publication No. 6.

1998   *Old Russia in Modern America: A Case from Russian Old Believers in Alaska.* 3rd ed. Juneau: Alaska–Siberia Research Center, Publication No. 10.

2007   *Staraya Rossiya v Sovremennoy Amerike: Russkiye Staroobryadtsy na Alayske* [Old Russia in Modern America: Russian Old Believers in Alaska]. Juneau: Alaska–Siberia Research Center, Publication No. 15.

2009a "Staroobryadtsy na Rusi: istinnyye prichiny i predmet tserkovnogo raskola" [Old Believers in Russia: Causes and Reasons of the Church Schism], *Russkiy Vek (Russian Century)*, 4(18):38-43.

2009b "Staroobryadtsy na Alyaske" [Old Believers in Alaska], *Russkiy Vek (Russian Century)*, 5(19):71-75.

DOLITSKY, ALEXANDER B. and DAVID PLASKET
1985 "Subsistence, Environment and Society: New Directions in Ecological Anthropology," *Ultimate Reality and Meaning*, 8(2):105–122.

DOLITSKY, ALEXANDER B. and LYUDMILA P. KUZMINA
1986 "Cultural Change vs. Persistence: A Case from Old Believers Settlements," *Arctic*, 39(3):223–231.

DOLGIKH, BORIS O.
1964 *Problemy Etnographii i Antropologii Arktiki* [On the Problems of Arctic Ethnography and Anthropology], *Sovetskaya Etnographiya*, 4:76-90.

DOROFEEV, N.
1980 *Organizatsiya i rabota folklyornogo kollektiva na primere Zabaykalskogo semeyskogo narodnogo khora* [Structure and work of the folklore collective based upon the Trans-Baykal folk choir of *Semeyskikh*]. Moscow: Minkultura SSSR.

DURKHEIM, EMILE
1933 [1893] *The Division of Labor in Society*. New York: Free Press.

1965 [1915] *The Elementary Forms of Religious Life*. London: Collier Macmillan Publishers.

EATON, JOSEPH W.
1952 "Controlled Acculturation: A Survival Technique of the Hutterites," *American Sociological Review*, 17(3):331–340.

EISENSTADT, SHMUEL N., ed.
1964 *Readings in Social Evolution and Development*. New York: Pergamon Press Ltd.

1970 "Social Change, Differentiation, and Evolution," *American Sociological Review*, 29:375–86.

2004 "Social Evolution and Modernity: Some Observations on Parsons's Comparative and Evolutionary Analysis: Parsons's Analysis from the Perspective of Multiple Modernity," *The American Sociologist*, 35(4):5–24.

ELIASOV, L. YE., ed.
1963 *Folklyor Semeyskikh* [Folklore of *Semeyskikh*]. Ulan-Ude.

FIRTH, RAYMOND
    1951   "Religious Belief and Personal Adjustment," *The Journal of the Royal Anthropological Institute of Great Britain and Ireland,* 78(1&2):25-43.

FORTIER, ED
    1970   "New Alaskan of Nikolaevsk," *Alaska,* November 1970, pp. 33-38.

FRAKE, CHARLES O.
    1962   "Cultural Ecology and Ethnography," *American Anthropologist,* 64:53-58.

FREEMAN, L.C. and R.F. WINCH
    1957   "Societal Complexity: An Empirical Test of a Typology of Societies," *American Journal of Sociology,* 62:461-466.

ILICHEV, L.F., ed.
    1982   *Materialisticheskaya dialektika kak obschaya teoriya razvitiya* [Dialectic Materialism as a General Theory of Development]. Moscow: Nauka.

GERSCHENKRON, ALEXANDER
    1970   *Europe in the Russian Mirror: Four Lectures in Economic History* London: Cambridge University Press.

GRINKOVA, N.P.
    1930   "Odezhda Bukhtarminskikh Staroobryadtsev" In: *Bukhtarminskiye Staroobryadtsy* ["Clothing of the Bukhtarmin Old Believers," In: *Bukhtarmin Old Believers*], Rudenko, S.I., ed. Leningrad: AN SSSR, 17:313-396.

GRUNWALD, CONSTANTIN DE.
    1962   *The Churches and the Soviet Union.* New York: McMillon.

GURVICH, ILYA S., ed.
    1980   *Etnogenez Narodov Severa.* [Ethnogenesis of the People of the North]. Moscow: Nauka.

    1982   *Etnicheskaya Istoriya Narodov Severa.* [Ethnohistory of the People of the North]. Moscow: Nauka.

HARRIS, MARVIN
    1968   *The Rise of Anthropological Theory: A History of Theories of Culture.* New York: Columbia University.

    1974   *Cows, Pigs, Wars, and Witches: The Riddle of Culture.* New York: Random House.

HELMS, MARY W.
1978   "Time, History, and the Future of Anthropology: Observations on Some Unresolved Issues," *Ethnohistory*, 25(1):1–13.

HERETZ, LEONID
2008   *Russia on the Eve of Modernity: Popular Religion and Traditional Culture under the Last Tsars*. Cambridge: Cambridge University Press.

HOSTETLER, JOHN A.
1965   "The Amish Use of Symbols and Their Function in Bounding the Community," *The Journal of the Royal Anthropological Institute of Great Britain and Ireland*, 94(1):11–21.

KEESING, FELIX M.
1963   *Cultural Anthropology: The Science of Custom*. New York: Holt, Reinehart and Winston.

KLYUCHEVSKY, VASILIY O.
1960 [1913] *A History of Russia*. Translated by C.J. Hogarth. London: J.M. Dent & Sons, Ltd.

KURLAND, J. and S. BECKERMAN
1985   "Optimal Foraging and Hominid Evolution: Labor and Reciprocity," *American Anthropologist*, 87(1):73–93.

KUZMINA, LYUDMILA P.
1982   "Ethnocultural Aspects of Research in the Oral Tradition of the Russian Population of Siberia," *Review of Ethnology*, 8:126–131. Wein: E. Stiglmyar.

1983   "Intercontinental and Regional Contacts between European and Non-European Cultures." Paper presented at the International Conference of Ethnicity, New Orleans, Louisiana, U.S.A., March, 1983, Moscow Institute of Ethnography, U.S.S.R., pp. 12.

LENSKI, G.
1966   *Power and Privilege: A Theory of Social Stratification*. New York: McGraw-Hill.

MALINOWSKI, BRONISLAW
1931   "Culture" In: *Encyclopedia of the Social Sciences*. New York: MacMillan, 4:621–646.

MAMSIK, T.S.
1975   *Obshchina i Byt Altayskikh Begletsov "Kamenshchikov"* [Community and Lifestyle of the Altay *Wonderers-Kamenshchikovs*]. In: *History and Traditions of the Siberian Peasant Families from the XVIIth to the Beginning of the XXth Centuries*. Novosibirsk: University Press, pp. 25–46.

MATROS, A.
   1827   *Pisma o Vostochnoy Sibiri* [Letters about East Siberia]. Moscow.

MERTON, ROBERT K.
   1934   "Durkheim's *Division of Labor in Society*," *American Journal of Sociology* 40:319–328.

MICHELS, GEORGE
   1997   "The Place of Nikita Konstantinovich Dobrynin in the History of Early Old Belief," *Revue Des Estudes Slaves.* Tome Soixante-Neuvieme. Fascicule 1-2. Paris, LXIX/1–2, pp. 21–31.

MORGAN, L.
   1963 [1877]   *Ancient Society.* New York: World Publishing Co.

MORRIS, RICHARD A.
   1981   *Three Russian Groups in Oregon: A Comparison of Boundaries in a Pluralistic Environment.* Ph.D. Dissertation, University of Oregon, Eugene, Oregon.

   1982   "A Touch of Old Russia in Modern America: Scenes from the Old Believer Settlements." Paper presented to the Annual Conference, Rocky Mountain Association for Slavic Studies, April 22–24, 1982.

MOSCALENKO, A.T. and A.P. OKLADNIKOV, eds.
   1983   *Metodicheskiye i philosopfskiye problemy istorii* [Methodological and Philosophical Problems of History]. Novosibirsk: Nauka.

MUTH, ROBERT M.
   1985   *Structural Differentiation and Community Growth: A Case Study of Natural Resource Development and Social Change in Selected Alaskan Communities.* Ph. D. Dissertation, Seattle, University of Washington.

NARROL, RAOUL
   1956   "A Preliminary Index of Social Development," *American Anthropologist,* 58:687–715.

NISBET, ROBERT N.
   1969   *Social Change and History: Aspects of the Western Ideas of Development.* New York: Oxford University Press.

   1970   "Developmentalism: A Critical Analysis." In: *Theoretical Perspectives and Developments.* McKinney, John C. and Edward A. Tiryakian, eds., New York: Appleton-Century-Crofts.

PARSONS, TALCOTT
   1964   "Elementary Universals in Society," *American Sociological Review,* 29:339–57.

1966 *Societies: Evolutionary and Comparative Perspectives*. Englewood Cliffs, New Jersey: Prentice-Hall, Inc.

1971 *The System of Modern Societies*. Englewood Cliffs, NJ: Prentice-Hall.

POKROVSKY, M.N.
1933 *Brief History of Russia*. Translated by D.S. Mirsky. London: Martin Lawrence, Ltd.

POKROVSKY, N.N.
1974 *Antifeodalnyy Protest Uralo-Sibirskikh Krestyan: Staroobryadchestvo v 18 Veke* [Anti-feudal Protest of the Ural-Siberian Old Believers in the 18th Century]. Novosibirsk: Nauka.

POPOVA, A.M.
1928 *Semeyskiye: Zabaykalskiye Staroobryadtsy* [*Semeyskiye:* Trans-Baykal Old Believers]. Verkhneudinsk.

RADCLIFFE-BROWN, A.R.
1952 *Structure and Function in Primitive Society*. London: Cohen & West.

REARDEN, JIM
1972 "A Bit of Old Russia Takes Root in Alaska." *National Geographic*, 142(3):401–425.

1975 "The Old Believers: A Progress Report from Nikolaevsk," *Alaska*, October issue, pp. 7–9.

RINDOS, DAVID
1985 "Darwinian Selection, Symbolic Variation, and the Evolution of Culture," *Current Anthropology*, 26(1):65-88.

ROZEN, E.A.
1870 *Zapiski Dekabrista* [Notes of the *Decembrist* (Political Exile)]. Leipzig.

REUSCHEMEYER, D.
1974 "Reflections on Structural Differentiation," *Zeitschrift Fur Soziologie*, 3(3):279–294.

1977 "Structural Differentiation, Efficiency, and Power," *American Journal of Sociology*, 83:1–25.

SAHLINS, MARSHALL
1977 *Culture and Practical Reason*. Chicago: University of Chicago Press.

SAHLINS, M. and E. SERVICE
1960 *Evolution and Culture*. Ann Arbor: University of Michigan Press.

SCHEFFEL, DAVID Z.
  1989   "There Is Always Somewhere to Go: Russian Old Believers and
         the State." In: *Outwitting the State*, Peter Skalnik, ed. *Political Anthropology*
         New Brunswick and London: Transaction Publishers, 7:109–20.

  1990   "In Search of Poland's Old Believers," *Anthropology Today*, 6(5):2–8.

SCHNORE, LEO F.
  1958   "Social Morphology and Human Ecology," *American Journal of
         Sociology*, 63:620–634.

SMELSER, NEIL J.
  1959   *Social Change in the Industrial Revolution*. Chicago: University of
         Chicago Press.

  1963   "Mechanisms of Change and Adjustments to Change." In: Hoselitz,
         Bert F. and Wilbert E. Moore, eds., *Industrialization and Society*, New
         York: UNESCO.

SOLOVIEV, SERGEY M.
  1980   *History of Russia: The Character of Old Russia*. Translated and
         edited by Alexander V. Muller. Gulf Breeze, Florida: Academic
         International Press.

SPENCER, BERKLEY A.
  1967   *Stability and Change in an Intervillage System of Highland Guatemala*.
         Ph.D. Dissertation, Cornell University.

STEPNIAK, SERGEY M.
  1977 [1888] *The Russian Peasantry: The Agrarian Condition, Social Life and
         Religion*. Westport, Connecticut: Hyperion Press.

STEWARD, JULIAN H.
  1955   *Theory of Culture Change: The Methodology of Multilinear Evolution*.
         Urbana: University of Illinois Press.

  1956   "Cultural Evolution," *Scientific American*, 194:69–80.

STURTEVANT, WILLIAM C.
  1966   "Anthropology, History, and Ethnohistory," *Ethnohistory*, 13(1):1–51.

TAYLOR, EDWARD
  1958 [1871] *Primitive Culture*. 2 Volumes. New York: Harper Torchbooks.

TROYAT, HENRI
  1990   *Peter the Great*. Norwalk, Connecticut: The Easton Press.

TURNER, JONATHAN H.
  1981   "Emile Durkheim's Theory of Integration in Differentiated Social Systems," *Sociological Perspectives*, 24(4):379–391.

USPENSKY, M. I.
  1905   *"Staroobryadcheskoye Sochineniye XVIII Stoletiya ob Odezhde"* [Old Believers' Essay on Clothing in the 18th Century]. Moscow: *Otdeleniye Russkogo Yazyka i Slovestnosti Akademii Nauk*, 10(2):18-30.

VERNADSKY, GEORGE
  1969   *The Tsardom of Moscow 1547-1682*. New Haven, Connecticut: Yale University Press.

WALLWORK, ERNEST
  1984   "Religion and Social Structure in *The Division of Labor*," *American Anthropologist*, 86:43-63.

WALLIS, W.
  1952   "Values in a World of Culture," *American Anthropologist*, 54(1):143–146.

WARE, TIMOTHY
  1986   *The Orthodox Church*. Suffolk: Penguin Books.

WHITE, LESLIE
  1945   "History, Evolutionism and Functionalism: Three Types of Interpretation of Culture," *Southwestern Journal of Anthropology*, 1:221–248.

  1949   *The Science of Culture*. New York: Ferrar, Strauss.

  1959   *The Evolution of Culture: The Development of Civilization to the Fall of Rome*. New York: McGraw-Hill.

WIGOWSKY, PAUL J.
  1978   *Collection of Old Believers History and Tradition*. Hubbard, Oregon: 91 Elementary School.

WILLEY, G. and J. SABLOFF
  1974   *A History of American Archaeology*. San Francisco: W. H. Freeman and Co.

WOODCOCK, GEORGE and IVAN AVAKUMOVICH
  1968   *The Dukhobors*. London: Faber and Faber.

YOUNG, F. and I. FUJIMOTO
  1965   "Social Differentiation in Latin American Communities," *Economic Development and Cultural Change*, 13:344–352.

YOUNG, F. and R.C.D. YOUNG
  1973 *Comparative Studies of Community Growth*. Rural Sociological Society. Monograph no. 2. Morgantown, West Virginia: West Virginia University Bookstore.

ZENKOVSKY, SERGE A.
  1957 "The Russian Church Schism: Its Background and Repercussions," *The Russian Review*, 16(4):37–58.

ZHILKO, ALEXANDER and EDUARD MEKS
  1997 "Old Believers in Latvia: Past and Present," *Revue Des Estudes Slaves*. Tome Soixante-Neuvieme. Fascicule 1–2. Paris, LXIX/1–2, pp. 73–88.

GLOSSARY

Acculturation—the adoption of cultural traits, norms and customs by one society from another. The changes in practice or beliefs that can be incorporated in the value structure of the society, without destruction of its functional autonomy (Eaton 1952:339).

Amish—Swiss Mennonite bishop (1693), the founder of the sect of Mennonite followers of Amman that settled in North America in the late 19th century.

Arctic Circle—the line of latitude located at 66°33' north of the equator.

Arctic Region—under the United Nation's Environmental Protection Program, the southern limit of the Arctic region is generally maintained north of the 60th parallel, as defined by the eight circumpolar countries.

Assimilation—no clear line can be drawn between acculturation and assimilation processes. "Assimilation is the end-product of a process of acculturation, in which an individual has changed so much as to become dissociated from the value system of his group, or in which the entire group disappears as an autonomously functioning social system" (Eaton 1952:339).

***Austrian* faction**—"*Austrian* faction of the *popovtsy* itself underwent schism in the 1860s when its moderate lay leadership advanced the idea that the official church also worshipped God and not Antichrist" (Heretz 2008:65).

Avvakum—Archpriest Avvakum was the most instrumental and effective leader of the Old Believers; he was burned at the stake in 1682 after having been exiled for ten years and imprisoned for twenty-two years.

Barter—the type of product exchange where no money is exchanged. It is found in a variety of socio-economic systems and constitutes the sole type of exchange in the economically simplest systems.

Bespopovtsy—(Russian) priestless grouping or concord among Russian Orthodox Old Believers.

Black clergy—the higher clergy in Russia, called the *black clergy*, were all monks. They were the servants of the tsar.

Boyars—(Russian) members of the nobility that emerged in 11th-century Russia when native Slavs began to join the advisors of the great princes. In the 15th and 16th centuries, the *boyars* declined as a class and a new nobility of service was created. By the 18th century, the *boyars* and the new nobility were indistinguishable, since the *boyars* had also accepted obligations of service (Cook 1990:42).

Braga—(Russian) a homemade, mildly alcoholic drink made from raisins, yeast, sugar, and berries.

Church Slavonic—two Greek brothers Cyril and Methodius invented the Slavonic alphabet in order to translate the Bible and service books so that services could be conducted in Slavonic. In their translation (AD 863), the brothers used Macedonian dialect spoken by the Slavs around Thessalonica. Thus, the dialect of the Macedonian Slavs became *Church Slavonic*, which remains the liturgical language of the Russian and certain other Slavonic Orthodox Churches, including Russian Old Believers in Alaska (Ware 1986).

Control acculturation—the process by which one culture accepts a practice from another culture, and integrates the new practice into its own existing value system (Eaton 1952:338).

Culture change—the process by which some members of a society revise their knowledge and use it to generate and interpret new forms of social behavior through innovation, social acceptance, performance, and integration processes.

Culture traits—the units or minimal features of socially transmitted behavior or handiwork. Each culture comprises tens of thousands of created or borrowed traits.

Diffusion—the spread of cultural features beyond the community in which it originated.

Dukhobor—(*Dukhoborets* in Russian) a member of the Russian sect originating in the 18th century that emphasizes the supreme authority of inner experience, that believes in the embodiment of the Spirit in different persons whom it follows as prophets and leaders, and that rejects all external ecclesiastical and civil authority to do military service or pay taxes.

Dvoeperstiye—(Russian) the sign of the cross with two fingers rather than three (the latter being the proposed reform) signified the dual nature of Christ from Father to Son.

Endogamy—the restrictive customs according to which a mate can be sought, or is preferably sought, only within one's own segment of the population. There are racial, religious, class, and other endogmatic rules.

Ethnic group—a group of people who share the same language, customs, and traditions.

Ethnogenesis—the search for ethnogenetic relations; a historical continuity or transformation of one cultural tradition into another in an attempt to discover the traits found in certain ethnic traditions and the historical origins of these traits.

Ethnography—the scientific description of the socio-economic systems and cultural heritage.

Folklore—the orally transmitted stories, tales, and myths rendered in a literary style.

Gregorian Calendar—the Gregorian Calendar is internationally the most widely used civil calendar. It is named after Pope Gregory XIII, who introduced it in October 1582. The calendar was a refinement to the Julian Calendar, involving a 0.002% correction in the length of the year.

Hutterites—a Mennonite sect (1536) of northwestern United States and Canada, living in small cohesive communities and holding property in common. Since the death of their namesake Jakob Hutter in 1536, the beliefs of the Hutterites, especially living in a cohesive community of goods and absolute pacifism, have resulted in hundreds of years of diaspora in many countries. Nearly extinct by the 18th and 19th centuries, the Hutterites found a new home in North America. Over 125 years, their population grew from 400 to around 42,000. Today, most Hutterites live in Western Canada and the Upper Great Plains of the United States.

Julian Calendar—the Julian Calendar, introduced by Julius Caesar in 46 BC (708 AUC), was a reform of the Roman calendar. It took effect in 45 BC (AUC 709), shortly before the Roman conquest of Egypt. It was the predominant calendar in the Roman world, most of Europe, and in European settlements in the Americas and elsewhere, until it was refined and gradually replaced by the Gregorian Calendar, promulgated in 1582 by Pope Gregory XIII. "Up to the end of the First World War, all Orthodox still used the Old Style or Julian Calendar, which is at present thirteen days behind the New or Gregorian Calendar. The Churches of Jerusalem, Russia and Serbia, together with the monasteries on the Holy Mountain of Athos, continue to this day to follow the Julian reckoning" (Ware 1986:308–9).

Kazak(s)—(Russian) free peasants and border guards of Russia and Ukraine. *Kazaks* are predominantly East Slavic-speaking people who became known as members of democratic, self-governing, semi-military communities located in Ukraine and Russia along the lower Dnieper, Don, Terek, and Ural river basins. They played an important role in the historical and cultural development of both Russia and Ukraine.

Liturgy—this is the term used by Orthodoxy to refer to the services of Holy Communion or the Mass.

Nastavnik—(Russian) a mentor, preceptor or instructor of apprenticies.

Nachyotchik—(Russian) a person well-read in Scriptures of the ancient Orthodox books.

Nastoyatel—(Russian) a layman or superior leader who is elected by the Russian Old Believer community as the spiritual leader.

Nikon—Patriarch Nikon proposed to correct the Holy Texts by introducing changes in the Church Books and the method of worship practiced by the Russian masses.

Orthodoxy—from the Greek *orthos* and *doxa*, 'true belief' considers that it was founded directly by Jesus. The word 'Orthodoxy' has the double meaning of 'right belief' and 'right glory.' The Orthodox regards their church as the church which guards and teaches the true belief about God and which glorifies Him with right worship (Ware 1986).

Popovtsy—(Russian) priestly grouping or concord among Russian Orthodox Old Believers.

Raskol—(Russian) the word *raskol* simply means a schism. In the context of Russian historical literature, the *raskol*, however, refers to the Russian Church Schism of the 17th century. There were, and continues to be, other *raskols* or, rather, splits (schisms) within Russian Old Believer communities, but to a much lesser degree than the "Great Raskol" of the 17th-century Russia.

Raskolniki—(Russian) "schismatics" or people of the schism.

Remeslenniki—(Russian) craftsmen.

Sarafan (Russian) the traditional woman's dress of Old Believers in Alaska. It is an all-purpose piece of clothing, serving both as the everyday work dress and as the dress for formal occasions.

Semeyskiye—(Russian) from the Russian word *semya* (family, of the family). The Old Believers faction.

Shashmura—(Russian) a woman's cap covered with a kerchief.

Sobor—(Russian) this word means both 'church' and 'council'. Among Old Believers, churches or praying houses reflect the community's internal social division and religious identity.

Startsy—(Russian) elders.

Survival—in social anthropology, a feature of culture retained with meager or no functioning role, but which presumably functioned in a more significant way at an earlier time and hence points usefully, for purposes of historical perspectives, to earlier cultural forms.

Taboo—a customary restraint or prohibition of certain words, items, or actions.

Talichka—(Russian) a non-traditional Russian dress, a variation of sarafan adapted in China. Talichka is never worn in church by Russian Old Believers.

Tolk—(Russian) religious affiliation or faction.

Trans-Baykal—mountainous region to the east of or "beyond" (trans-) Lake Baykal in southern Siberia.

Troeperstiye—(Russian) the three-fingered sign was intended as an acknowledgement of the Holy Trinity. This was considered by the conservative dissenters to represent Greek heresy.

Tsar—(Russian) emperor of Russia. An adaptation of the Roman 'Caesar'. Ivan the Terrible (1530–84) was the first to take the title of *Tsar*. He is known both as Ivan III and Ivan IV.

Ustavnik or ustavshchik—(Russian) is a law keeper; it is his job to keep track of the forms which the church service must take according to the ancient religious books.

Yedinovertsy—(Russian) monobelievers.

White clergy—the lower clergy and the servants of the villagers in Russia. No member of the *white clergy* could hope for promotion to places of power and wealth, such as bishoprics and archbishoprics, since these were the monopoly of the *black clergy*.

APPENDIX

Old Believer Holy Days for 2015 (7523) Orthodox Old-Rite Church Calendar

January
7 The Nativity of Christ (Christmas)[a,b]
8 Synaxis of the Mother of God
14 St. Basil the Great
19 The Holy Theophany of the Lord[a]
20 Synaxis of St. John the Baptist

February
12 The Three Holy Bishops
15 The Presentation of Christ[a]
19 Great Fast until April 7

April
1 Palm Sunday
7 Annunciation of the Mother of God[a]
8-14 Easter Week[a,b]

May
2 Mid-Pentecostal Wednesday[a]
6 The Great Martyr George
17 The Ascension of the Lord
21 St. John the Theologian[a]
22 Transfer of the Relics of St. Nicholas[a]
27 Pentecost Day of the Holy Trinity
28 Day of the Holy Spirit[a]

June
3 Vladimir Icon of the Mother of God[a]
4 Remembrance of the Holy Fathers[a]

July
6 Our Lady of Vladimir
7 Nativity of St. John the Baptist[a]
12 Saints Peter and Paul[a,b]
21 Our Lady of Kazan
23 Deposition of the Robe of Christ in Moscow
28 Saint Vladimir the Great

August
2 The Holy Prophet Elias
10 Our Lady of Smolensk
14 The All-Merciful Savior
19 The Transfiguration of Christ[a]
28 The Dormition of our Holy Mother of God[a,b]
29 The Image of Christ "Not Made by Hands"

September
8 Our Lady of Vladimir
11 The Beheading of St. John the Baptist[a]
21 The Nativity of the Mother of God[a]
27 The Exaltation of the Holy Cross of the Lord[a]

October
9 St. John the Theologian
14 The Protection of the Mother of God[a]

November
4 Our Lady of Kazan
21 The Holy Archangel Michael
26 St. John Chrysostom
28 Christmas fast begins until January 7

December
4 The Presentation of the Mother of God into the Temple[a]
19 St. Nicholas the Wonderworker[a]

---

[a] Indicates those days on which work is strictly forbidden; these are known as the "Great Feasting Days." [b] Indicates that this is the end of a Lenten fasting period. The Christmas Lent is 6 weeks long and Easter Lent runs 7 weeks; altogether Lenten fastings are 20 weeks in total.

INDEX

A

acculturation, v, ix, 2, 17, 65, 66
Alaska, iii, iv, v, vi, viii, ix, 9, 22, 25, 27, 28, 30, 32, 34, 35, 40, 42, 44, 45, 47, 49, 50, 53, 54, 56, 57, 58, 61, 66, 68
Alberta, 25
Altay Mountains, 17, 31, 59
Amish, 1, 35, 47, 59, 65
Anchor Point, 22, 25, 54
Antichrist, 12, 13, 15, 16, 56, 65
appearance, 14, 15, 18, 34, 37, 40, 54
Archpriest, 13, 14, 65
Arctic, iii, iv, 17, 51, 55, 57
Arctic Circle, 65
Arctic Region, iii, 65, 80
Argentina, 21
assimilation, vii, viii, ix, 65
Australia, 21
Austrian faction, 27, 30, 65,
Avvakum (Archpriest), 13, 14, 65

B

barter, 65
Baykal, Lake (*see* also Lake Baykal), 17, 18, 27, 30, 34, 37
banya, 34
Basargin, Fedor, 35, 38, 41
Beguny (priestless Old Believer branch), 27
Belokrinitsky Hierarchy, 25
Belorussia, vii, 17, 34
Berezovka (Old Believer village in Southcentral Alaska), 25, 54, 79
bespopovtsy (priestless Old Believer concord), 24, 25, 27, 31, 33, 65
black clergy, 13, 65, 69
Bolivia, 21
boyars, 34, 65
boundary maintenance, iv, 49, 50, 54
braga, 28, 29, 34, 66
Brazil, 21, 47
bride, 30, 31, 33, 34
Bukhtarmin Old Believers (reside in Altay Mountains), 31, 55, 58

C

Canada, iii, vii, 3, 21, 25, 47, 67
China, 5, 18, 21, 22, 40, 42, 47, 69
Church Slavonic, 11, 27, 44, 66
cohesive village, community or union, iii, vii, viii, ix, 22, 25, 49, 54, 67
controlled acculturation, 57

73

ABOUT THE AUTHOR

The Old Believer Andron Martushev (left) and the author Alexander B. Dolitsky (right),
Berezovka *village, Alaska, May 1986.*

Alexander B. Dolitsky was born and raised in Kiev in the former Soviet Union.
He received an M.A. in history from Kiev Pedagogical Institute, Ukraine in 1976;
an M.A. in anthropology and archaeology from Brown University in 1983; and
attended the Ph.D. program in anthropology at Bryn Mawr College from 1983 to
1985, where he was also a lecturer in the Russian Center. In the U.S.S.R., he was
a social studies teacher for three years and an archaeologist for five years for the
Ukrainian Academy of Sciences. In 1978, after living one year in Europe (Austria
and Italy), he settled in the United States. Dolitsky visited Alaska for the first time in
1981, while conducting field research for graduate school at Brown. He then settled
first in Sitka in 1985 and later in Juneau in 1986. From 1985 to 1987, he was the
U.S. Forest Service archaeologist and social scientist. He was an Adjunct Assistant
Professor of Russian Studies at the University of Alaska Southeast from 1985 to
1999; Social Studies Instructor at the Alyeska Central School, Alaska Department
of Education and Yukon-Koyukuk School District from 1988 to 2006; and President
of the Alaska–Siberia Research Center (AKSRC) from 1990 to present. He has

conducted 32 field studies in various areas of the former Soviet Union, Central Asia, South America, Eastern Europe and the United States. Dolitsky has been a lecturer on the *World Discoverer, Spirit of Oceanus* and *Clipper Odyssey* vessels in the Arctic and Sub-Arctic regions. He was the Project Manager for the World War II Alaska–Siberia Lend Lease Memorial, which was erected in Fairbanks in 2006. He has published extensively in the fields of anthropology, history, archaeology, and ethnography. His more recent publications include: *Fairy Tales and Myths of the Bering Strait Chukchi; Tales and Legends of the Yupik Eskimos of Siberia; Ancient Tales of Kamchatka; Old Russia in Modern America: A Case from Russian Old Believers in Alaska; Allies in Wartime: The Alaska–Siberia Airway During World War II; Spirit of the Siberian Tiger: Folktales of the Russian Far East; Living Wisdom of the Far North: Tales and Legends from Chukotka and Alaska;* and *Pipeline to Russia: The Alaska–Siberia Air Route in World War II.*